FAMILY LAW

CONTINUING LEGAL EDUCATION

6 Hours CLE Credit • 1 Hour Ethics Credit

JACKSON, MS • OXFORD, MS • GULFPORT, MS

ONLINE ON DEMAND

26ᵀᴴ ANNUAL
BELL FAMILY LAW CLE
SUMMARY OF CONTENTS

Family Law Developments: 2021 Cases 1

Youth Court/Chancery Court Children's Matters. 55

Rights Between Cohabitants 105

Parental Relocation in Mississippi 121

Collaborative Law and Ethics Issues 129

Appendix A 164

FAMILY LAW DEVELOPMENTS
TABLE OF CONTENTS

I.   Grounds for divorce 5
   A. Habitual, cruel, and inhuman treatment..5
     1. Unnatural and infamous conduct..5
     2. Spousal domestic abuse: Suit filed prior to effective date........5
     3. Standard of review...5
     4. Conflict in testimony 6
     5. Proof sufficient to grant divorce 6
   B. Desertion..7
   C. Task force recommendation: Unilateral no-fault divorce 8

II. Rights between cohabitants: Replevin 8

III. Property division 8
   A. Classification 8
     1. Basic rules of classification...8
     2. Separate property: Burden of proof 9
     3. Conversion of separate property through commingling and family use....9
     4. Separate property businesses 10
     5. Marital property cutoff date 10
   B. Valuation..11
     1. Pensions 11
     2. Valuation of items as a group...11
     3. Date of valuation 11
   C. Division 12
     1. Findings of fact 12
     2. Marital misconduct 12
     3. Unequal division based on need and contribution 13
     4. Assignment of debt 14
     5. Dissipation of assets..14

IV. Agreements...14

V.   Alimony 15
   A. Reversal with property division reversal...15
   B. Armstrong findings of fact...15
   C. Permanent alimony after short marriage 15
   D. Rehabilitative award inadequate..16
   E. Alimony properly denied...16
   F. Modification..17

VI.   Custody and visitation 18

  A. Pleadings 18

  B. Challenge to sole custody 18

  C. Custody between parents 18

    1. Presumption against custody to violent parent 18

    2. Child's preference 18

    3. Findings of fact 19

    4. Continuity of care 19

    5. *Albright* analysis 20

    6. Legal custody/decision-making 22

    7. Visitation 22

  D. Custody modification..23

    1. Modification during pending appeal 23

    2. Modification based on relocation...23

    3. Modification based on parental alienation 24

    4. Based on joint custodian's failure to communicate 24

    5. Modification based on adverse circumstances; no material change 25

    6. Modification of joint legal custody 25

    7. Modification of visitation..25

  E. Custody between parents and nonparents..26

    1. Temporary custody without notice..26

    2. Based on abandonment or desertion, including nonsupport 26

    3. Based on neglect 28

  F. Grandparent visitation 28

  G. Scope of *Albright* evidence on remand..30

  H. Guardians ad litem...31

    1. Mandatory guardians 31

    2. Scope of investigation...31

  I. Immunity for good faith reports of abuse or neglect............................32

VII. Child support...32

  A. Income for purposes of child support...32

    1. Findings of fact...32

    2. Military benefits..32

    3. Imputing income 32

  B. Family standard of living..33

  C. Deviation from the guidelines 33

  D. Add-ons to basic child support 34

    1. Health insurance and medical expenses.......................................34

    2. Extracurricular activities 34

  E. Cost of visitation 35

     F.   Tax deductions 35

     G.   Modification..35

         1. While child is in boarding school 35

         2. Reasonableness of custodial parent's choices 35

         3. Retroactivity...36

         4. Increase in support 36

         5. Decrease in support...36

             (a) Based on custody modification 36

             (b) Denied: No change in standard of living..37

     H.   Termination of support 37

VIII. Enforcement 38

     A. Property division..38

     B. Contempt 39

         1. Willfulness 39

         2. Failure to pay not willful 39

         3. Technical violation 40

         4. For withholding visitation..40

     C. Defenses to enforcement 40

         1. Disagreement with court orders 40

         2. Statute of limitations 40

     D. Incarceration for criminal contempt 41

IX.   Paternity 41

     A. Statute of limitations..41

     B. Presumption of paternity: Inheritance 42

     C. Presumption of paternity: Genetic testing 42

X.   Youth court proceedings...42

     A. Durable legal custody 42

     B. Youth court procedure and notice of rights 43

XI.   Termination of parental rights 44

     A. Physical abuse..44

     B. Substance abuse...44

     C. No contact with child...45

XII.   Adoption 45

XIII. Guardianships and conservatorships 46

XIV. Procedure 46
    A. Service of process 46
    B. Motions to recuse 46
    C. Trials 47
        1. Right to trial 47
        2. Judicial notice 47
        3. Evidence 48
        4. Attorney-client privilege 48
    D. Post-trial motions 48
        1. Motion for findings 48
        2. Motion to set aside judgment for fraud on the court 49
        3. Clarification of unclear order 49
    E. Appeals 50
        1. Time period for notice of appeal 50
        2. Contempt pending appeal 51
        3. Right to appeal *in forma pauperis* 51
        4. Failure to cite authority 51

XV. Attorneys' fees 51
    A. Findings of fact 51
    B. Review with remand of financial awards 52
    C. Sanctions 52
    D. Guardian ad litem fees 52

XVI. Tort actions 52
    A. Conversion of separate property 52
    B. Employer liability for husband's actions 53
    C. Malicious prosecution 54

FAMILY LAW DEVELOPMENTS

I.   GROUNDS FOR DIVORCE

A. Habitual, cruel, and inhuman treatment

1. Unnatural and infamous conduct

Roley v. Roley, 329 So. 3d 473 (Miss. Ct. App. 2021). The court of appeals affirmed a chancellor's grant of divorce to a wife based on habitual, cruel, and inhuman treatment. The wife and two witnesses testified regarding her husband's hoarding, extreme lack of cleanliness and personal hygiene, uncontrolled anger, verbal abusiveness, and physical violence. She and their children would not use the downstairs level of their home because of his hoarding. He would not allow them to throw away anything, including expired food. He once retrieved expired food from the trash and fed it to one of the children, who became ill. He screamed at his wife for small matters such as throwing out a used deodorant container. He did not bathe with soap, brush his teeth regularly, or wash his hands before preparing food. He punched holes in the wall and was physically abusive on one occasion. He told his young children that their mother was evil and did not love them. She testified that her husband's anger and explosiveness caused her emotional distress, that she was afraid of him, and that his hoarding and personal hygiene were so repulsive that she could not live with him. The wife and witnesses also testified that he allowed their ten-year-old son to watch pornography.

The chancellor found that the husband's verbal abuse, hoarding, lack of personal hygiene, and uncleanliness were so unnatural and infamous as to make the marriage revolting to the wife and make it impossible for her to discharge the duties of marriage. The court of appeals affirmed, rejecting the husband's argument that his wife failed to show harm because she offered no medical or psychological testimony. She presented sufficient evidence for the chancellor to determine that her husband's actions directly affected and endangered her physical health and well-being. Expert testimony is not required to prove that a defendant's behavior impacted a plaintiff.

2. Spousal domestic abuse: Suit filed prior to effective date

Roley v. Roley, 329 So. 3d 473 (Miss. Ct. App. 2021). The court of appeals clarified application of the new divorce ground of spousal domestic abuse, holding that the ground applied to an action filed before the effective date of the new ground but tried after the effective date.

3.   Standard of review

* *Roley v. Roley,* 329 So. 3d 473 (Miss. Ct. App. 2021). The court of appeals opted to apply the abuse of discretion standard to review divorces based

on habitual, cruel, and inhuman treatment even though a Mississippi Supreme Court decision states that the ground is reviewed de novo as a question of law. The court of appeals noted that the case on which the supreme court decision relied did not discuss the standard of review.

4. Conflict in testimony

Rankin v. Rankin, 323 So. 3d 1073 (Miss. 2021). The supreme court held that the court of appeals should have deferred to a chancellor's findings regarding habitual, cruel, and inhuman treatment. The wife testified that during their ten-year marriage her husband berated and emotionally abused her in private and in front of his church congregation. She testified that he physically abused her dog, pushed her during an argument when she was pregnant, kicked a suitcase into her, broke into her locked bathroom to continue an argument, called her derogatory names, and took the children away overnight because she would not have sex with him. She stated that the abuse caused her to have migraines and elevated blood pressure. Her husband admitted most of the incidents but characterized them as "pastor intense fellowship" and denied intending to hurt his wife. The chancellor found that the wife failed to prove habitual cruelty. The court of appeals reversed, holding that the wife presented sufficient evidence, if believed, to establish a pattern of emotional abuse that affected her health. The court of appeals noted that was no indication that the chancellor found her testimony lacking in credibility.

The supreme court reversed the court of appeals. Because there was a conflict in testimony, the court of appeals should have assumed that the chancellor resolved credibility issues against the wife. Two justices dissented, arguing that the difference in testimony was not about facts -- the husband admitted most of the incidents. According to the dissent, the couple differed in their subjective view of the husband's intentions and the emotional impact on his wife.

5. Proof sufficient to grant divorce

Kerr v. Kerr, 323 So. 3d 462 (Miss. 2021). A chancellor properly granted a husband divorce based on habitual, cruel, and inhuman treatment and denied his wife's petition for divorce on the same ground. Three witnesses, including the wife's father, testified that they observed her violent behavior toward her husband and others. The husband's parents saw her strike her husband repeatedly, once while holding their son. Her father sought to have her involuntarily committed after she reported that her husband had abused her. The father said that she attacked him, scratched him, hit him, and screamed at him. In addition, evidence showed that their toddler son ingested Klonopin while in her care. The court of appeals held that there was sufficient evidence to support the grant of divorce to the husband. The court also noted that abuse of a child may constitute cruelty toward the child's parent. The court affirmed denial of the wife's request for divorce, finding that her accusations of physical abuse were not credible. No person, including her father, supported her testimony.

Thornton v. Thornton, 324 So. 3d 345 (Miss. Ct. App. 2021). A chancellor properly granted a wife of thirty-five years a divorce based on habitual, cruel, and inhuman treatment. She testified that her husband called her "the devil" and "dumb" in front of their daughters. He objected to her attending college. He believed it was God's will that she submit to his decision that she should not gain an education or work. When she did secure a teaching position, he retaliated by refusing to support the household. She worked three jobs to pay household bills. Her husband had four cars but refused to allow her to drive them. He was physically violent on occasions, including one that her daughter witnessed and corroborated. In the three years prior to their separation, the couple lived in separate rooms and her husband refused to speak to her. He disabled their washing machine and toilet to harass her and refused to allow delivery men to remove a broken refrigerator to install a new one.

The court of appeals held that there was sufficient evidence of conduct that rose above the level of unkindness, rudeness, or incompatibility, corroborated by the plaintiff's daughter. Corroborating evidence need not be enough to prove the ground, only to convince the trier of fact that the plaintiff's testimony is true. Her testimony also proved a causal connection between his conduct and the injury to her – she testified that she was afraid for her safety. The court rejected the husband's argument that the clean hands doctrine barred his wife from divorce because she allegedly wasted marital assets and falsely accused him of giving her an STD. He waived the issue of unclean hands by failing to raise it at trial.

B. Desertion

*Stephenson v. Stephenson, 332 So. 3d 360 (Miss. Ct. App. 2021). The court of appeals overruled a 1940 Mississippi case stating that a husband has the right to determine family residence and that a wife's refusal to follow him is desertion. In the instant case, the couple separated after a few months of marriage when the husband was transferred to a work site an hour's drive from their home. He chose to move to be close to his job. His wife did not want to relocate. Four years later, the husband filed for divorce based on desertion, arguing that under *Ouzts v. Ouzts,* 199 So. 76, 78 (Miss. 1940), a wife must "acquiesce in his selection and follow him to the domicile of his choice unless the choice has been unreasonably and arbitrarily exercised."

The court of appeals relied on *Orr v. Orr*, 440 U.S. 268 (1979) to hold that *Ouzts* is no longer good law. The United States Supreme Court held in *Orr* that traditional notions of a man's responsibility to provide a home do not justify family law doctrines that discriminate based on gender. The court of appeals also agreed with the chancellor that even if *Ouzts* was good law, the husband's unilateral decision to move from their debt-free home and leave his wife behind was not made in good faith. Two judges dissented. In their view, the issue should be whether one spouse's decision to move or stay is unreasonable, regardless of gender. Because the husband was the family wage-earner, they argued, his decision to move was in good faith and his wife's refusal to follow him was unreasonable.

C. Task force recommendation: Unilateral no-fault divorce

Family Law Task Force. The Mississippi legislature authorized appointment of a fifteen-person task force to study and make recommendations for legislative changes in divorce grounds, child support, support for adult disabled children, and other matters related to family law. S.B. 2621 (2021). The Task Force Report, filed December 1, 2021, recommended that the Mississippi legislature adopt a true no-fault ground for divorce that does not require the agreement of both spouses.

II. RIGHTS BETWEEN COHABITANTS: REPLEVIN

Massey v. Neely, 309 So. 3d 138 (Miss. Ct. App. 2021). A circuit court judge properly entered a replevin order requiring a man's former girlfriend to return items related to cowboy-mounted shooting (guns, equipment, and clothing). He testified that he left the items in her trailer when the relationship ended because she agreed to bring them to an event they both planned to attend. When they did not attend the show, he arranged for a friend to meet her in Meridian to retrieve the items. She told the friend she would deliver them herself. At trial, however, she argued that the items were gifts to her. The chancellor found that the items belonged to the plaintiff and entered an order of replevin. In post-trial motions, the woman argued that venue for a replevin action lies in the county of the defendant's residence or where the items are located. The court agreed that venue was improper initially but held that she waived the issue when she failed to raise it as an affirmative defense and participated in the trial. The court also agreed with the defendant that the plaintiff failed to provide evidence of the value of each item as required by the replevin statute. However, she failed to raise the issue until after the trial. In addition, she testified that each of the items on the list were in her possession.

III. PROPERTY DIVISION

A. Classification

1. Basic rules of classification

- There is a presumption in favor of marital property. All property held by a divorcing couple is presumed to be marital and divisible regardless of title.
- The spouse claiming that an asset is separate, in whole or in part, has the burden of proof.
- An asset is separate if it was acquired prior to marriage, after the cutoff date for marital property, as a gift or inheritance, or is excluded by agreement.
- The cutoff date for marital property accumulation may be as early as separation or as late as divorce.

- Appreciation caused by marital efforts is marital property. Passive appreciation of separate property is separate; passive appreciation of marital property is marital.
- *Some* separate property may be converted to all marital if
    (a) marital funds are commingled into the property; or
    (b) the property is used for family purposes.

Converted*	Not converted: Tracing allowed
Marital home	Retirement accounts
Real property	Businesses
Bank accounts	

* A minority line of cases permits tracing separate interests in these assets.

2. Separate property: Burden of proof

Lageman v. Lageman, 313 So. 3d 1075 (Miss. Ct. App. 2021). A husband argued unsuccessfully that a chancellor erred in classifying his entire retirement account as marital even though he allegedly made premarital contributions to the account. The burden of proof is on the spouse who claims that an asset is separate. The husband provided no evidence of the premarital value of the account. The court also rejected his argument that he should have been credited with amounts attributable to his premarital interest in a home that he owned for eighteen months prior to the marriage and which was sold after the couple lived there for four years. He provided no information on the premarital value of the house or information about how the sale proceeds were used.

Doe v. Doe, No. 2020-CA-00853-COA, 2021 WL 5193082 (Miss. Ct. App. Nov. 9, 2021). The court of appeals held that a chancellor erred in classifying a husband's life insurance policies as marital. He introduced bank statements proving that his mother paid all premiums on two premarital life insurance policies in his name. When a spouse proves that an asset is premarital the burden shifts to the other spouse to prove that the asset was converted to marital property. The wife offered no proof to contradict his evidence that all premiums during the marriage were paid with separate funds.

3. Conversion of separate property through commingling and family use

In re Conservatorship of Geno, No. 2018-CA-01767-COA, 2021 WL 1184583 (Miss. Ct. App. March 30, 2021). A chancellor properly found that a husband's $3,352,000 Vanguard account was a mixed asset, classifying the premarital value of $893,190 and passive growth of $322,403 on the premarital value as the husband's separate property. The fact that the husband made additional contributions to the account during marriage did not convert the account to marital through commingling. The court cited *Brock v. Brock,* 906 So. 2d 879 (Miss. Ct. App. 2005), for the proposition that "The key to determining when there has been transmutation by commingling is whether the marital interest can be identified, i.e., can be traced." The court also rejected the wife's argument that the account was converted to marital because the husband used withdrawals to pay family expenses. The court distinguished a prior case in which a husband commingled disbursements from his IRA into marital accounts and actively managed the IRA. In this case, the husband used funds from the account to pay household expenses but there was no evidence of commingling into marital accounts and he did not actively manage the account. The chancellor properly classified a portion of the account as separate by tracing the funds to premarital contributions.

The court also affirmed the chancellor's treatment of the $298,808 premarital value of a retirement account as separate. All funds contributed during the marriage were classified as marital.

4. Separate property businesses

*In re Conservatorship of Geno, No. 2018-CA-01767-COA, 2021 WL 1184583 (Miss. Ct. App. March 30, 2021). The court of appeals affirmed a chancellor's separate classification of a husband's LLC. Prior to his marriage, he created an LLC to hold title to an office building. The LLC expenses were paid with rent from tenants, including the husband's law practice. The court of appeals rejected the wife's argument that the LLC was a marital asset because the husband's law practice paid rent to the LLC. The husband received no income from the LLC, no marital funds were commingled in the business, and the LLC assets were not used for family purposes.

5. Marital property cutoff date

*Coleman v. Coleman, 324 So. 3d 1204 (Miss. Ct. App. 2021). A chancellor properly divided a couple's assets and declined to award a disabled husband alimony or attorneys' fees. The husband received $1,500 a month in Social Security disability. His wife had net income of $2,781 from her job as a school psychologist. The husband was awarded the marital home, cattle, a lawnmower, and vehicles. The wife was awarded her retirement account and her vehicle and ordered to pay her student loan debt. The court properly classified a home purchased by the wife after the couple's separation as her separate property, even though the bank required that she put her husband's name on the deed. A court has discretion to set the date on which marital property accumulation ceases as early as the date of separation. The wife obtained the loan and made the mortgage payments with her post-separation income. The husband quitclaimed his interest in the house to her and made no contributions toward the purchase. The court also rejected the husband's argument that he should have been credited with the value of a $13,000 life insurance payment that he contributed to the marital home. He presented no proof of the payment.

B. Valuation

1. Pensions

Lageman v. Lageman, 313 So. 3d 1075 (Miss. Ct. App. 2021). The court of appeals affirmed a chancellor's classification and division of a husband's FedEx pension as a mixed asset. The husband began working for FedEx as a handler six years before the couple married. During their marriage he became a pilot with a higher monthly adjusted income of $21,386. He had worked for FedEx for twenty-four years at the time of trial. The wife earned $2,972 working four days a week as an occupational therapist. Neither party provided evidence of the pension's value or proof to identify the separate portion of the pension. The chancellor speculated that his annual contributions in the first six years were substantially less than the amount of his annual contributions during the marital years. In recognition of the six years of premarital contributions, the chancellor awarded the husband 55% of the pension. The court of appeals rejected the husband's argument that the chancellor erred in failing to value his pension or classify the separate portions. He provided no evidence on the issue and in fact did not disclose his pension as an asset on his Financial Statement. Given the limited information available to the court, the chancellor's ruling was a proper way to classify and divide the account.

2. Valuation of items as a group

Doe v. Doe, No. 2020-CA-00853-COA, 2021 WL 5193082 (Miss. Ct. App. Nov. 9, 2021). The court of appeals held that a chancellor erred in valuing personal property in a lump sum of $30,000 without valuing individual items. The items included a boat, fishing equipment, tractor, four-wheeler, golf cart, furniture, appliances, and computers. The court based the $30,000 value on the wife's testimony that the fishing equipment was worth $20,000 and the husband's tools worth $15,000. No values were given for the boat, golf cart, furniture, or appliances. Considering the high value placed on the group of items, the chancellor should have required the parties to provide evidence of each item's value and assigned possession of each item, stating the value assigned to each.

3. Date of valuation

Bowman v. Bowman, 332 So. 3d 317 (Miss. Ct. App. 2021). A chancellor did not err in ordering a wife to repair and sell a Mercedes automobile and divide the proceeds of the sale with her husband. She was awarded temporary possession of the vehicle three years earlier in the court's temporary order. The court rejected her husband's argument that the chancellor should have awarded him half of the higher value of the car at the time of separation. Chancellors have discretion to set valuation dates. It is not necessary to value all items on the same date. The court also noted that in general, it is better to value property closer to the date of divorce.

C. Division

1. Findings of fact

Bowman v. Bowman, 332 So. 3d 317 (Miss. Ct. App. 2021). The court of appeals rejected a husband's argument that a chancellor's property division should be reversed for failure to conduct a *Ferguson* analysis. Although the chancellor did not explicitly discuss the factors, he considered the parties' contributions, whether they had dissipated assets, and determined the value of properties. The court also noted that several *Ferguson* factors were irrelevant given the short marriage length and the couple's premarital agreement.

However, the court held that the chancellor erred in finding that it was impossible to determine the parties' contributions to joint banking accounts. The husband and wife shared a joint checking account with a $1,005 balance and a joint savings account containing $79,282. The chancellor divided the accounts equally after stating that their individual contributions could not be determined. The court of appeals agreed with the husband that his expert's report showed that he made significantly more contributions. He deposited $162,873 directly into the savings account, while the wife made no deposits into the account. The court reversed for the chancellor to reconsider division of the savings accounts in light of the husband's greater contributions.

Doe v. Doe, No. 2020-CA-00853-COA, 2021 WL 5193082 (Miss. Ct. App. Nov. 9, 2021). The court of appeals reversed and remanded a chancellor's property division based on its holding that the chancellor erred in findings of fact. In dividing the couple's assets, the chancellor found, based in part on judicial notice, that the husband transmitted an STD to his wife. The court of appeals reversed, holding that the court erred in making findings related to medical conditions based on judicial notice. The court instructed the chancellor to reassess the *Ferguson* factors in light of the reversal on those findings.

2. Marital misconduct

Hammond v. Hammond, 327 So. 3d 173 (Miss. Ct. App. 2021). The court of appeals reversed a chancellor's property division awarding a wife 55% of the marital estate, for failure to consider her husband's adultery in the *Ferguson* analysis. The couple's twenty-five-year marriage ended when the wife discovered her husband's ongoing affair. The revelation contributed to her depression and damaged the husband's relationship with their children. The husband's net monthly income was $12,150. The forty-seven-year-old wife, who had been a homemaker for twenty years, earned $646 a month as a preschool assistant. The court divided the marital assets with 55% to the wife and 45% to the husband. The husband was ordered to pay $1,167 in child support and rehabilitative alimony of $500 a month for two years, in addition to paying his wife's health insurance for two years. The court of appeals agreed with the wife that the chancellor erred in failing to consider the husband's adultery in the *Ferguson* analysis. A chancellor must consider marital misconduct that affects the stability and harmony of a marriage in dividing the couple's assets. The husband's adultery ended the marriage, caused his wife's depression, and affected his children. He spent $10,000 on his paramour during the marriage. The court also held that an award of $500 a month in alimony for two years was grossly inadequate under the circumstances.

Coleman v. Coleman, 324 So. 3d 1204 (Miss. Ct. App. 2021). A chancellor properly divided a couple's assets and declined to award the disabled husband alimony or attorneys' fees. The court of appeals held that the chancellor did not err in finding that the husband's marital misconduct – inappropriate communication with other women – was a cause of disharmony in the marriage and considering his conduct as a factor in property division.

3. Unequal division based on need and contribution

Lacoste v. Lacoste, 313 So. 3d 1097 (Miss. Ct. App. 2021). On the second appeal of a court's property division, the court of appeals held that a chancellor properly valued and divided the couple's marital estate. In the first trial the chancellor valued the husband's fitness training business based on the previous year's profits minus debts and adding the value of the company's few assets. The chancellor awarded the wife 54% of the assets and 83% of the debts and the husband 46% of the assets and 17% of the debts. The husband was also ordered to pay his wife a $73,000 equalizing payment. The court of appeals reversed, holding that the chancellor erred in her valuation of the business based on the previous year's profits. In the second trial, the chancellor valued the business at $13,900, based on expert testimony using the net asset method, rather than the $347,417 value assigned in the first trial. The court of appeals noted that the expert's valuation properly excluded goodwill as required in divorce valuations. The chancellor awarded the husband his business, removed the $73,000 lump sum payment, and left the remaining division of assets intact. As a result, the wife received 91% of the assets and 90% of the debt. The husband appealed, arguing that the division was inequitable. The court emphasized that equitable does not mean equal and that chancellors have substantial discretion in dividing marital assets. The chancellor supported the unequal division by finding that the wife had no income, that she had participated in her husband's business, and that she made a significant contribution to family life. An equal division would have left her without sufficient assets to meet her needs. The division avoided the need for alimony or to award her a portion of the husband's business and made it possible for the wife to pay off the debts assigned to her.

Pace v. Pace, 324 So. 3d 369 (Miss. Ct. App. 2021). The court of appeals affirmed a chancellor's unequal division of marital assets. The chancellor ordered that the wife sell the marital home, the husband's medical practice building, and other items with a total value of approximately $1,000,000. She was directed to divide the proceeds equally with her husband after payment of expenses. The chancellor awarded her the remaining asset of $120,000 in cash. The court of appeals rejected the husband's argument that the cash should have been divided equally. The wife was unemployed and had custody of their son. She had worked for her husband's medical practice before he relinquished his license to practice rather than pay for monitoring following treatment for substance abuse. In addition, the husband's earning capacity far exceeded hers.

4. Assignment of debt

Doe v. Doe, No. 2020-CA-00853-COA, 2021 WL 5193082 (Miss. Ct. App. Nov. 9, 2021). A chancellor erred in assigning an $18,000 debt, incurred to pay family expenses, solely to the husband. The chancellor initially ordered that the spouses share responsibility for the debt but amended the order post-trial to require the husband to pay the debt. No reason for the change was stated. The court of appeals noted that debts incurred for family purposes are marital and stated that nothing in the record supported allocation of the full debt to the husband. On remand, the chancellor should allocate half to each spouse or provide a reason for an alternate division.

5. Dissipation of assets

In re Conservatorship of Geno, No. 2018-CA-01767-COA, 2021 WL 1184583 (Miss. Ct. App. March 30, 2021). The court of appeals reversed a chancellor's property division for findings of fact regarding a wife's dissipation of assets. The court held that the chancellor erred in finding that the wife dissipated $200,000 in marital assets without making specific findings of fact, when the husband presented evidence that she dissipated $595,269 in assets. It was not possible to determine what funds the chancellor considered dissipated without more specific findings.

IV.   AGREEMENTS

Bowman v. Bowman, 332 So. 3d 317 (Miss. Ct. App. 2021). The court of appeals affirmed a chancellor's interpretation of a couple's ambiguous premarital agreement. Prior to their three-year marriage, the couple executed a premarital agreement with contradictory provisions. Section 2 stated that assets purchased during the marriage with premarital assets would remain separate. Section 4 provided that jointly titled assets acquired during marriage would be marital property. At issue were three properties acquired with the husband's premarital funds but titled in both parties' names. The chancellor found that the provisions were contradictory but that the agreement was enforceable and classified the properties as marital. The court of appeals noted that in the event of an ambiguity, courts should first apply the canons of construction to resolve the ambiguity. Two canons supported the chancellor's decision: First, an ambiguity should be read more favorably for the non-drafting party, in this case the wife. Second, a specific provision should be given more weight than a general provision. Both supported a finding that section 4 controlled. Applying section 4, jointly titled property purchased during marriage with the husband's premarital funds should be classified as marital.

Hatton v. Hatton, 323 So. 3d 1149 (Miss. Ct. App. 2021). A chancellor properly declined to address division of a couple's only significant asset, the marital home, based on their prenuptial agreement. The parties, both in their seventies, had been married seven years. They executed a premarital agreement which provided that their premarital property would remain separate. They also agreed that any assets acquired as joint tenants with rights of survivorship would pass to the survivor and would remain in joint title. The agreement provided, "Neither party shall attempt at any time to sever such joint tenancy, unless mutually agreed upon by the parties." During the marriage, they purchased a home titled as tenants by the entirety with rights of survivorship. The wife asked that the home be sold and the proceeds divided. The husband asked for sole ownership. The chancellor granted a divorce based on irreconcilable differences and held that the premarital agreement was an enforceable contract. The chancellor declined, based on the agreement, to award exclusive possession of the home to either party. Because disposition of the only marital asset was governed by the premarital agreement, the chancellor found it unnecessary to address the *Ferguson* factors. The court of appeals affirmed.

V. ALIMONY

A. Reversal with property division reversal

Doe v. Doe, No. 2020-CA-00853-COA, 2021 WL 5193082 (Miss. Ct. App. Nov. 9, 2021).

The court of appeals declined to consider a husband's argument that a chancellor erred in not awarding him alimony. Because the property division was remanded, the issue of alimony should be reconsidered on remand.

B. *Armstrong* findings of fact

Warren v. Rhea, 318 So. 3d 1187 (Miss. Ct. App. 2021). The court of appeals affirmed a chancellor's award of $750 a month in rehabilitative alimony for four years to a wife of fifteen years, based on the disparity in the couple's incomes. Her adjusted gross income was between $1,200 and $2,115 a month. The husband's gross income was $4,795. The court rejected the husband's argument that the chancellor's failure to address the *Armstrong* factors required reversal. Failure to address the factors does not require reversal if the record contains facts from which the court can determine that the award was proper. The chancellor considered the marriage length, the parties' contributions to the marriage, and the disparity in their incomes.

C. Permanent alimony after short marriage

In re Conservatorship of Geno, No. 2018-CA-01767-COA, 2021 WL 1184583 (Miss. Ct. App. March 30, 2021). The court of appeals affirmed a chancellor's award of $2,500 a month in permanent alimony to a thirty-eight-year-old wife of seven years, who suffered from mental health issues, had been hospitalized for treatment, and was under a conservatorship. Her husband had $1.5 million in separate assets. The wife received $1.25 million in cash and a debt-free house. The court rejected her argument that the award would not allow her to live at the standard of living of the marriage – because of the husband's reduction in income, neither would be able to live at their prior standard of living. The court also rejected the husband's argument that the award was excessive because of the wife's age, the short term of the marriage, and her dissipation of assets. She had no income and her illness and need for treatment supported the award. However, because property division was remanded for findings of fact on dissipation, the chancellor was free to revisit alimony on remand. Property division and alimony are linked – where one expands, the other may recede.

D. Rehabilitative award inadequate

* *Hammond v. Hammond*, 327 So. 3d 173 (Miss. Ct. App. 2021). The court of appeals reversed a chancellor's property division granting a wife 55% of the marital estate for failure to consider her husband's adultery in the *Ferguson* analysis. The court also reversed the award of $500 a month in alimony for two years as inadequate. The couple's twenty-five-year marriage ended when the wife discovered her husband's ongoing affair. The husband's net monthly income was $12,150. He received an annual bonus of $67,938 the previous year. The forty-seven-year-old wife, who had been a homemaker for twenty years, earned $646 a month as a preschool assistant. The chancellor divided the marital assets with 55% to the wife and 45% to the husband. The husband was ordered to pay $1,167 in child support and rehabilitative alimony of $500 a month for two years, in addition to paying his wife's health insurance for two years. The court of appeals remanded the case for the chancellor to review the *Ferguson* factors in light of the husband's marital misconduct. The court also held that an award of $500 a month in alimony for two years was grossly inadequate under the circumstances. The marriage was long and the disparity in their financial resources great. There was no evidence that the wife could earn substantially more than she was earning. She had been a homemaker by the parties' joint decision and the marriage ended because of her husband's misconduct. The court remanded for the chancellor to consider an appropriate lump sum or periodic alimony award. The court held, however, that the chancellor did not err in limiting the husband's obligation for her health insurance to two years or in refusing to award her remaining attorneys' fees of $3,675.

E. Alimony properly denied

Pace v. Pace, 324 So. 3d 369 (Miss. Ct. App. 2021). The court of appeals held that a chancellor properly denied alimony to a forty-three-year-old wife of thirteen years. She was in good health, had a college degree, and was a registered nutritionist. She received one-half of the marital assets valued at approximately $1,000,000 and an additional $120,000 in cash in the property division.

Coleman v. Coleman, 324 So. 3d 1204 (Miss. Ct. App. 2021). A chancellor properly divided a couple's assets and declined to award the disabled husband alimony or attorneys' fees. The husband, who was injured on the job, received $1,500 a month in Social Security disability. The wife had net income of $2,781 as a school psychologist. The court rejected his argument that the court erred in finding that the division of assets adequately provided for both parties without undertaking an analysis of the *Armstrong* factors for awarding alimony. When a chancellor determines that property division adequately provides for both spouses, an *Armstrong* alimony analysis is not necessary.

F. Modification

Braswell v. Braswell, 336 So. 3d 1121 (Miss. Ct. App. 2021). A chancellor erred in denying a father's motion to reduce alimony – he suffered a significant loss in income because of a substance abuse problem and as a result of Covid. At divorce, the ophthalmologist father, who was earning $280,000 a year, agreed to pay $2,500 a month in child support for one child and $4,500 a month in alimony to his wife of twenty-six years. Three years later he experienced financial stress when his dentist brother moved out of their jointly owned office building. The father began to drink heavily, was given a DUI, and was suspended from practice until he completed in-patient treatment. The licensure board required that he limit his practice to four-day weeks for five years. The father sought a reduction in support, claiming that he lost income because of his brother's move, his inability to practice for two months, his required limitation of hours, and the mandatory Covid shutdown. His home and business were foreclosed or sold, he filed for bankruptcy, and his income dropped to $54,363 a year in 2019. He lived in a house purchased by his current wife and her grandmother, with a monthly rental payment of $600. He did not take vacations or continue his previous lifestyle. He used his stimulus check to pay child support arrearages, had no assets, and was behind on taxes. The chancellor found that his income loss caused by drinking was voluntary and not a material unforeseeable change in circumstances. He also found that the pandemic shutdown did not rise to the level of a material and substantial change in circumstances.

The court of appeals distinguished the case relied on by the chancellor, noting that the husband's drinking in that case predated the divorce and was not a material change. In this case, the husband's stress-induced drinking began two years after the divorce. The resulting practice limitation imposed by the licensure board was involuntary. To follow the chancellor's logic, "no modification could be granted to a person whose reckless behavior leads to a loss of income." The court also held that the mandated office closure due to Covid was a material change in circumstances. The cumulative effect of these changes caused a drastic reduction in the father's income and his ability to pay alimony. The court remanded for the chancellor to determine an appropriate amount of alimony but held that child support should be terminated because the child now lived with the father.

VI. CUSTODY AND VISITATION

A. Pleadings

Johnson v. Smith, No. 2019-CA-01450-COA, 2021 WL1381090 (Miss. Ct. App. April 13, 2021). The court of appeals affirmed a chancellor's order granting parents joint legal and physical custody for eleven months until their child started school, then continuing joint legal custody but with physical custody in the father. The court rejected the mother's argument that the chancellor erred in awarding the father sole custody because he requested only joint physical custody. The original petition asking for custody and general relief was sufficient to encompass sole custody as a form of relief. A chancellor may grant a form of custody that was not specifically requested if that is in the child's best interest. The mother also argued that she was deprived of due process because she lacked notice that the issue of sole custody would be tried. However, the issue was tried by consent and without objection at trial.

B. Challenge to sole custody

Roley v. Roley, 329 So 3d 473 (Miss. Ct. App. 2021). A pro se father who was granted supervised visitation every other Sunday and telephone visitation three days a week argued unsuccessfully that *Albright* lacks a scientific basis. He contended that children are best served by joint physical custody. The court of appeals noted that it lacked authority to overrule the supreme court's established custody rules and declined to address his argument.

C. Custody between parents

1. Presumption against custody to violent parent

Kerr v. Kerr, 323 So. 3d 462 (Miss. 2021). The supreme court affirmed a chancellor's award of custody to a father, holding that the presumption against custody to a parent with a history of family violence did not apply. The chancellor found that the wife's allegations of her husband's abuse were not credible. Because the presumption was not triggered, the chancellor was not required to make findings of fact regarding rebuttal of the presumption. Nor was the chancellor required to consider domestic violence in applying the *Albright* factors, based on his finding that the husband was not abusive.

2. Child's preference

Roley v. Roley, 329 So. 3d 473 (Miss. Ct. App. 2021). The court of appeals declined to consider a father's argument that a Mississippi statute allowing courts to consider the preference of children over twelve violates the free speech rights of younger children. The issue was procedurally barred because the father did not make a proffer of the children's testimony. And, the two prerequisites to considering a child's preference were not met. The statute provides that a chancellor must find that both parents are fit persons to have custody and are able to provide for the children before considering a child's preference. The chancellor found that the father was not fit to take custody.

3. Findings of fact

Polk v. Polk, 332 So. 3d 348 (Miss. Ct. App. Nov. 23, 2021). A divided court of appeals affirmed a chancellor's award of custody to a mother even though the chancellor did not discuss the evidence related to the *Albright* factors. The judgment listed the factors and stated a conclusion for each. The majority noted that the chancellor's bench opinion discussed the evidence under the factors in detail. The majority disagreed with the dissent's position that failure to discuss the evidence under each factor required reversal.

4. Continuity of care

* *Johnson v. Smith,* 328 So. 3d 145 (Miss. Ct. App. 2021). The court of appeals affirmed a chancellor's modification of custody of a sixteen-year-old boy from his mother to his father. When the couple divorced in 2014, the mother had custody of the boy and his younger sister. However, after the mother moved to another school district, she brought the children to the father's house every morning where they caught the bus. In the afternoons, they returned to his house for the afternoon, did homework and had dinner, then went to the mother's house to sleep. The son spent most of his days during the summer at his father's house. Both children lived full time with the father when the mother moved to Texas for three months. When she returned, the son refused to return to her home for four months. The father petitioned for modification of custody of the son and modification of child support.

The chancellor found that a material change in circumstances had occurred, based on the mother's frequent arguments with her son, including once locking him out of the house. The son asked to live with his father, stating that he felt unsafe at his mother's house but that his father supported him instead of yelling at him. The court of appeals held that the chancellor did not err in finding for the father on continuity of care, even though the mother had custody. The father had provided most of the care for his son, even if he slept at the mother's home. Nor did the chancellor err in finding against the mother on the factors of moral fitness and mental health. She argued frequently with her son, locked him out of the house, moved to Texas and did not communicate with the children for four months. The father was also favored on the home, school, and community record of his son, who attended school where the father lived. The father helped him with homework, attended school events, and the boy stated that he considered it his home. Stability of the home environment also favored the father, who had the same job for seventeen years, lived in the marital home, and provided a safe, calm environment.

5. *Albright* analysis

Kerr v. Kerr, 323 So. 3d 462 (Miss. 2021). A chancellor did not err in finding that the age of a four-year-old boy was neutral but that his sex favored his father. Nor did the chancellor err in finding the factor of continuity of care to be neutral. Although the mother was the primary caregiver prior to separation, the father was the primary caregiver during separation. Chancellors are allowed to consider post-separation care even though *Albright* states the factor as "continuity of care prior to separation." The father was favored on parenting skills, considering the mother's lack of patience with her son and that the boy had missed thirty-two days of daycare during her custodial time. The father was also favored on willingness to provide childcare and employment responsibilities – he was employed and working to provide for the boy, while the mother was unemployed. The father was favored on mental and physical health based on the mother's involuntary commitment and failure to pursue treatment for her anxiety disorder. The chancellor found for the father on the child's home, school, and community record because of the boy's excessive pre-school absences in her care. The chancellor also considered that the boy tested positive for Klonopin after being in his mother's care as a factor in awarding the father physical custody.

The supreme court disagreed with the mother's argument that the chancellor had no authority to order that the child attend daycare. The chancellor found that the boy would benefit from the education and socialization available at daycare and ordered that he attend for half days.

Embrey v. Young, No. 2021-CA-00091-COA, 2021 WL 5576070 (Miss. Ct. App. Nov. 30, 2021). The court of appeals affirmed a chancellor's award of seven-year-old and two-year-old children to their mother. The chancellor did not err in finding for the mother on the age of the younger child, who was two years old and breastfeeding. Nor did the chancellor err in finding for the stay-at-home mother on employment responsibilities rather than finding for the father who worked. The fact that the mother was living with her fiancé did not require finding against her on moral fitness, nor did the fact that she smoked marijuana during her first pregnancy eight years earlier. There was no evidence of current drug use. Furthermore, the father had previously been arrested for possession of marijuana. The chancellor properly found for the mother on parenting skills, based on the father's abusive language and treatment of her in front of the children, which the chancellor found to be "horrible parenting skills." Finally, the chancellor was not required to address the issue of separating the boys from their older half-sibling. The father waived the issue by failing to raise it at trial.

Bingham v. Johnson, 322 So. 3d 948 (Miss. Ct. App. 2021). A chancellor properly awarded custody of a three-and-a-half-year-old girl to her father. The factor of the child's age and sex slightly favored the mother. However, the chancellor found for the father on moral fitness, based on the mother's untruthfulness. She stated that she lived in a trailer that her cousin owned, but the place appeared to be abandoned. Her car was seen frequently outside the home of a male friend. The husband offered a video of her leaving the friend's house with the child at 5:15 in the morning. When confronted with a photograph of her kissing the man, she denied that she was the woman in the photograph. The chancellor also found for the father on stability of employment and home. It was unclear where the mother lived, while the father continued to live in the marital home where the child had her own room. The child's home, school and community record favored the father, who took the girl to church regularly and involved her in activities with extended family. The court did not err in finding the factor of continuity of care to be neutral. Even though the mother stayed home with the child for the first four months of her life, the father helped to care for the child and her stepsister after that and during the couple's separation.

Polk v. Polk, 332 So. 3d 348 (Miss. Ct. App. 2021). The court of appeals affirmed a chancellor's award of custody of a four-year-old boy to his mother, finding that substantial evidence supported the decision. The mother left the boy with his father in January of 2019 to move to South Carolina with her two older children. The father was granted temporary custody between that time and the trial in August 2020. The mother worked as a certified nurse assistant in South Carolina, where she had a three-bedroom home and lived with her two older children. The father lived with his parents, who helped to provide childcare while he worked. The chancellor found that both had good parenting skills, were morally fit, and were willing and able to provide childcare. The father was favored slightly on continuity of care and the child's home school and community record. The mother was favored slightly on stability of employment because her job was full-time and more secure. The mother was also favored slightly on emotional bond because of the boy's attachment to his two older half-siblings. Under "other factors" the court considered it a negative that the father had limited contact with his eight-year-old daughter from a prior relationship.

Tedford v. Tedford, 312 So. 3d 420 (Miss. Ct. App. 2021). The court of appeals affirmed a chancellor's award of custody to a father. The mother used marijuana, alcohol, and profane language in the children's presence and struck her husband on several occasions. The father was favored on children's health because he assisted one child with speech development issues. He was favored on parenting skills because the mother's older daughter had abused drugs and became pregnant at a young age. He was favored on employment because he worked while the mother was not employed. The court acknowledged that the factor of employment and ability to provide childcare can favor a parent who is at home or one who is employed – the chancellor did not err in choosing the latter. The court found against the mother on moral fitness because of her drug use, prior relationships, and history with her older daughter. The father was favored on the children's home, school, and community record because he enrolled the children in preschool and because of his extended family's daily involvement in church. Finally, he was favored on stability of the home because he had a home with bedrooms for the children while the mother's home needed substantial repair.

6. Legal custody/decision-making

Bryant v. Bryant, No. 2020-CA-00883-COA, 2021 WL 5802520 (Miss. Ct. App. Dec. 7, 2021), *cert. granted,* 336 So. 3d 652 (Miss. 2022). The supreme court in April 2022 granted certiorari on this case involving parental decision-making. The court of appeals affirmed a chancellor's modification of a couple's agreement regarding their children's education. When the couple divorced, one child attended private school in Hernando. Their twins were preschool age. The parents agreed to share joint legal and physical custody but provided that the father had final decision-making authority if they could not agree. A separate provision stated that each parent would pay for one-half of the older child's private school tuition. If either party was financially unable to afford tuition for the twins, the court "will reevaluate this matter upon Motion of either party." The agreement was later amended to modify physical custody to the mother but legal custody remained the same. When the twins were of school age, the father notified the mother that he planned to enroll all three children in the Lake Cormorant public school where his current wife taught. The mother petitioned the court to order that they be enrolled in the Hernando public schools where she and the children lived. The chancellor found that neither party could afford private school and that it was in the children's best interests to attend school where they lived rather than thirty minutes away.

The father argued that the chancellor's authority was limited to determining *whether* the parties were able to pay for private school and did not extend to ordering *what* public school they should attend. The majority agreed with the mother, stating that chancellors have final authority in children's matters and may modify an agreement to address the children's best interests. In addition, the agreement itself provided that the parties "agreed and understood" that the contract could be submitted to the court "for approval or disapproval."

The dissenting judges argued that the agreement did not give the chancellor authority to determine where the children attended school. The provision stating that the court could "approve or disapprove" the agreement was standard irreconcilable differences divorce language recognizing that the court had to accept the agreement. It did not give the court authority to revise the agreement later. The dissenters agreed that courts can modify provisions related to children if there is a material change in circumstances. In this case, however, the chancellor made no finding of a material change to justify limiting the father's decision-making authority.

7. Visitation

Myers v. Myers, 324 So. 3d 808 (Miss. Ct. App. 2021). A chancellor properly allowed a father unsupervised visitation with his daughters, finding no evidence to support the mother's repeated allegations that he had sexually abused one of the girls. Multiple reports to CPS were unsubstantiated. Police investigators testified that they found no evidence of abuse. Repeated interviews with the girl produced no statement regarding abuse and the court-appointed counselor observed a health interaction between the father and child.

Roberts v. Conner, No. 2019-CA-01782-COA, 2021 WL 2429490 (Miss. Ct. App. June 15, 2021). The court of appeals affirmed a chancellor's order limiting a mother's visitation to Mississippi, where she had extended family with whom she could stay. The evidence at trial showed that her home in Florida was unlivable.

Warren v. Rhea, 318 So. 3d 1187 (Miss. Ct. App. 2021). The court of appeals reversed and remanded a chancellor's award of custody for failure to summarize the mandatory guardian ad litem's report. The court also held that a visitation award without a specific schedule is error, and instructed the chancellor to revisit the schedule on remand.

D. Custody modification

1. Modification during pending appeal

Roley v. Roley, 329 So. 3d 473 (Miss. Ct. App. 2021). A chancellor denied a father's post-trial motion to modify visitation, stating that he had no authority to modify visitation while the matter was on appeal. The court of appeals held that a chancellor may modify visitation or custody while a matter is pending if the circumstances warrant. However, the father presented no evidence to support his argument that visitation should have been modified.

2. Modification based on relocation

Smith v. Smith, 318 So. 3d 484 (Miss. Ct. App. 2021). The court of appeals affirmed a chancellor's modification of custody and child support triggered by a custodial mother's move to enroll her daughter in a school to address learning disabilities. The parents of two children divorced in 2014, agreeing to joint legal custody, physical custody in the mother, and extensive visitation for the father. The father agreed to pay $1,000 a month in support for each child, one-half of the children's tuition at their current private school and "any other such schools they may attend," health insurance, out-of-pocket medical costs, and any extracurricular activities on which both parents agreed. Two years later, their daughter was diagnosed with dyslexia and Expressive/Receptive Language Disorder. The parents agreed that the mother would move to Memphis to enroll her in a school for children with dyslexia in January 2017. Their son remained with his father in Jackson until the fall of 2017 when he enrolled at McCallie Preparatory School in Chattanooga. At the end of the 2018-19 academic year, he returned to Jackson to live with his father. In April of 2018, the mother decided to enroll the daughter in the Currey-Ingram School in Nashville, a move that the father objected to as unnecessary, disruptive to his relationship with his daughter, and too expensive.

The chancellor found that the mother's relocation from Memphis to Nashville was not a material change in circumstances that warranted modification of custody to the father. However, he did find that it required modification of visitation. The court of appeals rejected the father's request that the court revisit the Mississippi rule that a custodial parent's relocation is not, in itself, a material change in circumstances. The court stated that it lacked authority to overturn supreme court precedent.

3. Modification based on parental alienation

Davis v. Davis, 329 So. 3d 461 (Miss. Ct. App. 2021), *cert. granted,* 326 So. 3d 465 (Miss. 2021). The court of appeals reversed and rendered a chancellor's modification of custody from joint physical custody to sole custody in the father. The chancellor found a material change in circumstances based on two events: (1) the mother's report of physical abuse by the father was found to be unsubstantiated, and (2) the mother obtained DNA tests that showed a probability that another man was the child's biological father. On one occasion, the mother noticed bruising on the four-year-old girl's arms. The child said that her father "jerked her around." The mother filed a report of felonious child abuse after the girl came home from with bruises around her eye and said that her father struck her in the eye. The charge was dismissed for lack of evidence. The father testified that he was not the primary caregiver on the day she was bruised and that she was jumping on a trampoline that day. A forensic interviewer found that the bruises were more consistent with an accident than abuse. The guardian ad litem found no evidence of abuse and recommended custody in the father. The chancellor found that the mother's charges of abuse were without rational evidence and constituted a material change in circumstances. The chancellor also found that the mother's attempt to identify another man as the child's father was an intentional interference with the father's parental rights.

The court of appeals disagreed, holding that the mother's report was not baseless. And, although the charges were dropped, the child did repeat the same accusation to a forensic interviewer. The court also disagreed that the mother's contact with the child's possible biological father was a material change. There was no evidence that the girl was aware that another man could be her biological father.

4. Based on joint custodian's failure to communicate

Thornton v. Thornton, 322 So. 3d 485 (Miss. Ct. App. 2021). The court of appeals affirmed a chancellor's modification of custody of a couple's younger son from the mother to the father. The chancellor found a material change in the mother's home – she was in a relationship with a man convicted of armed robbery and aggravated assault who spend time with the boys; the younger son's grades had suffered; and the mother interfered with the father's rights and failed to meet her obligations as a joint legal custodian. She listed her boyfriend as an emergency contact instead of listing the father. She did not inform the father of the boy's failing grades, medical problems, or let him know about upcoming events. She enrolled the boy in a different school without telling the father and refused to allow visitation if he was delayed by work. The chancellor found that only continuity of care favored the mother. The father rated higher on physical and mental health, moral fitness, and the children's home school and community record. The court found that the boy's failing grades and absences and tardies in the mother's care was a negative under the home, school, and community record. The mother's failure to meet her obligations as a joint legal custodian weighed against her under "other factors."

5. Modification based on adverse circumstances; no material change

Croney v. Solangi, 328 So. 3d 749 (Miss. Ct. App. 2021). In the second custody appeal involving this family, the court of appeals affirmed a chancellor's modification of custody of a fourteen-year-old boy to his father. The parents' litigation spanned a decade after the mother was awarded custody in 2009. The father's 2015 petition to modify custody was denied but the chancellor awarded him extra visitation and ordered family counseling. Two years later, the father argued that a material change had occurred, citing the counselor's report that his son suffered from anxiety and depression and wanted to live with him. He also alleged that the mother attempted to limit his time with his son and to interfere with his ability to attend school events and to talk with his son by phone. The court-appointed guardian ad litem's report was consistent with the counselor's. Both recommended a change in custody, believing that the boy's mental health would improve if he lived with his father.

The chancellor found no material change in the mother's home but held that it was in the boy's best interest to live with his father, relying on the custody modification test set out in *Riley v. Doerner*, 677 So. 2d 740 (Miss. 1996). The chancellor found that the *Albright* factors of the child's preference, parents' age and health, and stability of home environment favored the father, while continuity of care favored the mother. The court of appeals affirmed. *Riley* held that in rare cases a court may modify custody without finding a material change in the custodial parent's home, if the existing arrangement is "actually detrimental to the child's well-being" and modification will advance the child's best interests.

6. Modification of joint legal custody

Smith v. Smith, 318 So. 3d 484 (Miss. Ct. App. 2021). A chancellor held that parents' inability to work cooperatively over three years required modification from joint legal custody to sole legal custody in the parent with physical custody of each child. The court of appeals affirmed – the parents could not agree on routine decisions and had filed numerous motions regarding the children's education.

7. Modification of visitation

Smith v. Smith, 318 So. 3d 484 (Miss. Ct. App. 2021). A chancellor found that a mother's relocation from Memphis to Nashville was a not a material change in circumstances that warranted modification of custody to the father but that it required modification of his visitation. The father was granted five weeks in the summer, two long visits each semester, alternating spring breaks, alternating holidays, and the option to visit his daughter in Nashville one weekend a month. The court rejected the father's argument that the chancellor's visitation order unduly limited his time with his daughter. Chancellors have broad discretion in setting a visitation schedule that works in the child's best interests.

Polk v. Polk, 332 So. 3d 348 (Miss. Ct. App. 2021). A court awarded custody of two children to a mother living in South Carolina, with the Mississippi father granted visitation. The court rejected the father's argument that his visitation was unduly restrictive. He was awarded spring, fall, and Thanksgiving breaks, a week at Christmas, most of the summer, a monthly weekend visit in South Carolina, and multiple weekly phone visits.

E. Custody between parents and nonparents

1. Temporary custody without notice

Roberts v. Conner, 332 So. 3d 272 (Miss. Ct. App. 2021). The court of appeals held that a chancellor did not err in granting petitioners (a deceased father's friends) temporary custody without notice to the child's mother. They alleged that the girl faced irreparable injury if she moved to Florida with her mother. She struggled in school during the mother's temporary custody but her grades improved in her father's care. Her mother traveled extensively and could not provide the girl with a stable environment. They feared the mother would abscond with the child to Florida if she had notice of the hearing. In the past, she had failed to return the girl to her father and was in violation of the order when the father died. She refused to allow the girl to visit with the father's family after his death.

2. Based on abandonment or desertion, including nonsupport

Summers v. Gros, 319 So. 3d 479 (Miss. 2021). The supreme court affirmed a chancellor's award of custody to grandparents rather than to a boy's mother. When the boy was four his mother agreed that he could live with his grandparents to attend a private school that they paid for. He spent weekends and holidays with her for a year. When the mother did not return him to the grandparents' home after a visit they sought and were granted temporary custody. The temporary order did not provide for visitation with the unrepresented mother. Four months later she was granted four hours visitation on Sunday, which she exercised for three months. Then she married, moved to Texas to live with her husband, and had a child. She did not visit with the boy for eighteen months, but then visited him once or twice a month. Three years after the temporary order, the chancellor granted permanent custody to the grandparents, finding that the mother failed to support her son and failed to exercise visitation frequently.

On appeal, the mother argued that it was error to award the grandparents temporary custody -- there was no showing of a problem in her home. The supreme court acknowledged that it had "reservations about the correctness of the temporary orders;" that the temporary order contributed to her failure to spend time with her son, and that the order had a practical, and perhaps a decisive, impact on the final custody decision. However, she failed to promptly attack the temporary order, waiting three months to petition for visitation and a year to prepare a visitation order. She did not file for contempt when the grandparents denied her visitation. The court also noted that the temporary order was moot because it was superseded by the custody decree.

The court of appeals held that the grandparents overcame the natural parent presumption. The mother deserted her son by failing to support him and failing to exercise visitation for extended periods of time. She paid no support to the grandparents until a child support order was entered and then failed to pay support regularly, making a lump sum payment the day before trial. She failed to exercise her half-day visitation for eighteen months after she moved to Texas and after that visited only once or twice a month.

Two justices dissented, arguing that the strong presumption in favor of natural parents should require custody to the mother where, as the majority agreed, the evidence could have supported a finding that she did not desert her son. They dissenters pointed out that when she was living in Mississippi and allowed visitation, she exercised her visitation at almost every opportunity.

In re T.D., 324 So. 3d 1187 (Miss. Ct. App. 2021). The court of appeals affirmed a chancellor's award of custody of four children to their maternal grandmother after their mother's death. Prior to their mother's death, the father would sometimes disappear for long periods. He did not provide for them financially. After her death, the children lived with him for a portion of a year until the grandmother sought and was granted custody. The chancellor found that the father had abandoned the children by his limited presence in their lives, his failure to support them, and his neglect of them while in his care. The natural parent presumption was rebutted by proof of immoral or unfit conduct, including his drug use, bringing multiple women to the home, and failure to take medication required for schizophrenia. The chancellor properly found that the grandmother was favored on the *Albright* factor of parenting skills. The father sent the children to school without supplies or books and in dirty clothes. They were often late or absent. The home deteriorated after the mother's death and was described as filthy. The guardian ad litem observed the younger children playing in the street unsupervised under the father's care. The court also found for the grandmother on ability to provide primary care. She worked in the mornings and could take the children to school, pick them up, and work with them on homework. She had a three-bedroom house with ample room for the children, while it was unclear where the father lived. She was favored on mental and physical health, based on the father's drug use and untreated schizophrenia. She was favored on moral fitness based on the father's drug use, arrests, and failure to support his children. The court rejected his argument that the court erred in failing to give him standard visitation. He had twice-monthly visitation for full weekends, a day at Christmas, and three hours on each child's birthday.

3. Based on neglect

Roberts v. Conner, 332 So. 3d 272 (Miss. Ct. App. 2021). The court of appeals affirmed a chancellor's award of custody to a deceased father's friends rather than the child's mother. When the couple divorced, the mother had temporary custody for two years during the separation. The father was awarded custody in the divorce.

The chancellor found that the petitioners overcame the natural parent presumption by proving that the mother was unfit, based on educational and medical neglect. The child had thirty absences and thirty-seven tardies in the mother's pre-divorce custody and had to repeat the first grade. She medically neglected the girl by cancelling a tonsil surgery and failing to reschedule it and by allowing her Medicaid to lapse and failing to secure other health insurance. The mother could not provide the court with an address at which she and the child would live in Florida. Her current home was infected with black mold. The mother's temporary residence in Mississippi was a two-bedroom home shared with six people and in which the girl slept in a recliner. Finally, the mother failed to meet the girls' basic needs. She did not bathe or brush her teeth regularly in her mother's care. Her mother cancelled dance lessons that the girl loved, stopped taking her to a counselor, and would not allow her to see her best friend after her father's death.

F. Grandparent visitation

*Greer v. Akers, No. 2019-CA-00745-COA, 2021 WL 248051 (Miss. Ct. App. Jan. 26, 2021). The court of appeals affirmed a chancellor's award of grandparent visitation with the oldest two of three sisters, but reversed visitation as to the youngest. The grandmother spent significant time, including some overnights, with the two oldest girls. She also spent time, including some overnights, with the youngest daughter until she was ten months old. At that point, the parents refused to allow the grandmother to see the girls after an altercation that resulted in the police arresting the girls' father. The chancellor found that the grandmother did not financially support the older girls but did have frequent visitation, including overnights, for more than a year. He also found that the grandmother's ten-month relationship with the youngest child substantially met the requirements of the statute. The court of appeals reversed the chancellor's finding that the grandmother had met the statutory requirement for a viable relationship with the younger child. The statute, which is strictly construed, requires frequent visitation for a period of not less than one year or financial support for six months or more, with regard to each child. The court held that the chancellor correctly applied the *Martin v. Coop* factors to find that visitation was in the best interests of the older children. The grandmother's home was suitable and near the family. She was of good moral character and responsible. She was able to care for them, in good health, had a loving relationship with them, and did not interfere with the parents' discipline. The court declined to follow the parents' request to develop additional *Martin* factors – a chancellor is free to consider any other relevant factors in addition to those listed in the case. The court also rejected the parents' argument that an award of one weekend a month and ten

consecutive days in the summer was excessive.

The parents argued that visitation with fewer than all siblings should be denied because there is a general principle against separating siblings in custody and visitation. The court held that the rule does not apply to grandparent visitation and suggested that the parents could alleviate the problem by sending the younger child to visit with her sisters.

One judge concurred, urging that the legislature amend the grandparent visitation statute to allow visitation for grandparents who can establish a viable relationship during the majority of an infant's life.

Battise v. Aucoin, 311 So. 3d 588 (Miss. 2021). The supreme court reversed a chancellor's award of attorneys' fees to a mother in a visitation action brought by the paternal grandmother. The grandmother sought visitation under MISS. CODE ANN. δ 93-16-3 after her son died. The chancellor awarded the mother $3,500 in attorneys' fees in advance of the hearing. On appeal, the supreme court held that the statutory provision for an award of attorneys' fees from grandparents applies only to Type 2 grandparent visitation, when the petitioner is seeking visitation against her own children. Subsection (4) of the statute, which provides for attorneys' fees refers to "petitions for visitation rights under subsection (2)." No similar provision refers to subsection (1) visitation, based on a child's death or loss of custody.

Sims v. Sims, No. 2020-CA-00327-COA, 2021 WL 3732944 (Miss. Ct. App. Aug. 24, 2021). A chancellor did not err in denying a paternal grandfather visitation with his four grandchildren. The grandfather had not established a viable relationship with the two youngest children and failed to prove that his son had unreasonably denied him visitation. The chancellor found that the grandfather had a viable relationship with the two older children, who had spent a substantial amount of time with him. However, the children's father cut off visitation not long after the two twin girls were born. A grandparent must establish a viable relationship with each individual child with whom he seeks visitation. The chancellor also rejected the grandfather's argument that his son unreasonably denied his visitation. The son, his brother, and his wife all testified that the grandfather was controlling, manipulative, and went into rages that sometimes became physical. The son testified that his father belittled and humiliated him as a child and attempted to control him even as an adult. In the last year, the son had observed similar behavior in his father's interaction with his three-year-old son. The court of appeals held that the parents had legitimate concerns about the grandfather's future conduct, including that the grandfather would disregard their decisions about discipline and engage in attempts to manipulate the children against their father. The court also rejected the grandfather's argument that the chancellor should have addressed the children's best interests before denying visitation. A chancellor is not required to move to a best interest analysis unless she first finds a viable grandparent-child relationship and that the parents unreasonably denied visitation. The court noted that a grandparent visitation action is "not a contest between equals." Parents have a paramount right "to control the environment, physical, social and emotional, to which their children are exposed."

G. Scope of *Albright* evidence on remand

Gossett v. Gossett, 313 So. 3d 1063 (Miss. Ct. App. 2021). A chancellor did not err in awarding temporary custody to a father or in converting the temporary award into permanent custody several years later. The father had served thirteen years for a 2002 murder conviction and was released in 2004. The couple married in 2007 and their daughter was born in 2011. Both parents filed for divorce based on adultery in 2015. The chancellor awarded the mother temporary custody, which was dissolved when the chancellor denied divorce in March 2016 without addressing custody. The child lived with her mother for the next two years pending the husband's appeal. The court of appeals remanded for the chancellor to reconsider his divorce grounds.

On July 31, 2018, the chancellor granted the husband a divorce based on adultery. At the remand hearing, the chancellor examined custody evidence presented at the March 2016 trial, without taking new evidence. He found that the father was favored on continuity of care, stability of employment, and stability of home environment. Because of concern that the father would interfere with the mother-child relationship, the chancellor awarded the father temporary custody, to be reexamined in six months. The six-month hearing was assigned to a new chancellor after the sitting chancellor retired. The new chancellor declined to reweigh the *Albright* factors but did hear evidence of circumstances occurring in the last six months, including the father's loss of employment. The chancellor awarded permanent custody to the father.

The court of appeals rejected the mother's argument that the first chancellor erred in awarding temporary custody to the father based on two-year-old evidence. The court noted that when a case is remanded, a party is not necessarily entitled to a new hearing unless it is mandated by the appellate court. In addition, the mother's Rule 59 motion to allow her to introduce newly discovered evidence (evidence between 2016 and 2018) was properly denied. The evidence she sought was not newly discovered evidence, which is evidence that did not exist at the time of the 2018 trial. Also, the order from which she sought relief was a temporary order and not a permanent award of custody – she was not entitled to relief under Rule 59. And finally, the evidence she sought to present was in fact considered at the July 2019 custody review hearing.

Roberts v. Conner, 332 So. 3d 272 (Miss. Ct. App. 2021). In a third-party custody action against a child's mother, a chancellor properly considered evidence that predated the parents' divorce decree. The mother had temporary custody of the girl pending divorce but the father was awarded sole custody at divorce. After his death, friends sought and were awarded custody of the girl over her mother. The chancellor properly looked to evidence of the mother's medical and educational neglect of the girl during her temporary custody prior to divorce.

H. Guardians ad litem

1. Mandatory guardians

Savell v. Manning, 325 So. 3d 1208 (Miss. Ct. App. 2021). A chancellor did not err in refusing to appoint a guardian ad litem based on a mother's general allegations that the father "failed to provide a safe environment" and that their child returned from a visit "in poor physical condition." She provided no specifics to support the allegation and did not allege abuse and neglect. Her report of abuse to CPS was determined unsubstantiated.

Embrey v. Young, No. 2021-CA-00091-COA, 2021 WL 5576070 (Miss. Ct. App. Nov. 30, 2021). The court of appeals held that a chancellor was not required to appoint a mandatory guardian ad litem. The father did not request a guardian, although he stated to the mother that her nephew had abused their older son. The court first learned of the allegations at trial. The father presented no specifics regarding the abuse. The child's therapist testified that the child's statements were inconsistent and that they indicated coaching by the father. DCPS found the claim to be unsubstantiated. The chancellor was not required to appoint a mandatory guardian ad litem when the father did not raise the issue at trial and the evidence presented did not support a legitimate issue of abuse.

Warren v. Rhea, 318 So. 3d 1187 (Miss. Ct. App. 2021). The court of appeals reversed and remanded a chancellor's award of custody for failure to summarize the mandatory guardian ad litem's report and to provide reasons for not following her recommendations. The guardian recommended that the father have custody of the couple's teenaged son, who had been physically and emotionally abused by his mother. The guardian recommended that she not be awarded visitation unless the boy's counselor determined that it was safe and in his best interest to visit with her. The chancellor awarded custody to the father and "reasonable visitation" to the mother. When a guardian is mandatory, a chancellor's decision must summarize the report and provide reasons for deviating from the guardian's recommendations.

2. Scope of investigation

Roberts v. Conner, 332 So. 3d 272 (Miss. Ct. App. 2021). The court of appeals rejected a mother's argument that a chancellor should have granted a continuance for the guardian to visit her home in Florida. All parties agreed that her prior home – and the only one available to inspect – was uninhabitable due to black mold. She failed show what information the guardian could have gained by a visit.

Summers v. Gros, 319 So. 3d 479 (Miss. 2021). A chancellor did not err in changing the designation of a guardian ad litem from an expert witness, providing instead that she would testify as a guardian ad litem. A chancellor's order of appointment for a guardian ad litem may be expanded or limited as the needs of the case require.

I. Immunity for good faith reports of abuse or neglect

The Mississippi legislature amended Miss. Code Ann. δ 43-21-355 to extend immunity for good faith reports of abuse or neglect to persons who participate in an investigation, evaluation, or judicial proceeding resulting from a report of abuse or neglect. The amendment also provides that members of a child advocacy center or multidisciplinary team acting in good faith and in the scope of their duties are not liable for damages for making or referring a report of abuse or neglect, conducting an investigation, making an investigative judgment, or releasing or using information to protect a child. H.B. 0356 (2021).

VII. Child support

A. Income for purposes of child support

1. Findings of fact

Jones v. Jones, No. 2020-CA-00923-COA, 2021 WL 5459436 (Miss. Ct. App. Nov. 23, 2021). A chancellor erred in modifying child support without evidence of the parents' incomes. The parties agreed at divorce that the noncustodial father would pay $600 a month in support for two children. The chancellor modified custody of the son to his father and reduced his support obligation for the daughter to $300 a month. He ordered the mother to pay $175 a month in support for the son. The court of appeals reversed, holding that the chancellor erred in determining child support without first ascertaining the parties' current incomes.

2. Military benefits

Jefferson v. Jefferson, 327 So. 3d 1085 (Miss. Ct. App. 2021). A father's gross income for calculation of child support included military benefits, specifically, payments for basic allowable subsistence, basic allowable housing, cost of living allowance, and clothing entitlements. The court of appeals rejected the father's argument that the chancellor erred in including these amounts. The child support statute provides that gross income includes "all potential sources that may reasonably be expected to be available to the absent parent." Miss. Code Ann. δ 43-19-101. The chancellor properly awarded 14% of the father's adjusted gross income as child support, even though he testified that he would soon be discharged from service and could not estimate his post-service income.

3. Imputing income

Pace v. Pace, 324 So. 3d 369 (Miss. Ct. App. 2021). A chancellor properly based an award of $1,200 a month in support for one child on a physician father's earning capacity as a doctor, rather than on his current income. After the couple separated, the father was required by the Mississippi Physician's Health Program to undergo in-patient treatment for substance abuse and to participate in a monitoring program to keep his license. He spent three months in treatment but relinquished his license rather than agree to monitoring. He argued that the $14,000 annual cost of monitoring was prohibitive. He also argued that he was disabled by a 2011 stroke; however, he presented no medical evidence of disability. The chancellor found that the wife provided him with funds to pay initial monitoring costs and that he had funds from property division to pay the fee in the future. The chancellor also found that the father could earn over $100,000 a year as a physician. The court of appeals affirmed, holding that a chancellor may base support on a payor's earning capacity, rather than actual income, when the payor has voluntarily reduced their income.

Smith v. Smith, 318 So. 3d 484 (Miss. Ct. App. 2021). The court of appeals rejected a father's argument that an unemployed noncustodial mother should have been ordered to pay child support based on her parents' regular and substantial gifts. The court distinguished cases in which a parent's family paid them a set monthly stipend or whose family paid their living monthly expenses. In addition, the court noted that the mother did provide support by paying one-half of the son's private school tuition, which her parents paid.

B. Family standard of living

Lageman v. Lageman, 313 So. 3d 1075 (Miss. Ct. App. 2021). A chancellor did not err in ordering a father with monthly adjusted income of $21,386, plus substantial annual bonuses, to pay $4,000 a month in support for two children. The court of appeals rejected his argument that the award was excessive since the wife listed the children's expenses as less than that amount. The court stated that the guidelines create a rebuttable presumption that a child support payor should pay twenty percent of his income for two children. If a payor's annual adjusted gross income is over $100,000, the chancellor must make a finding that application of the guidelines is reasonable. In addition, a chancellor may consider the family standard of living in setting child support. The court also noted that the wife's list of expenses did not include amounts for housing, utilities, and transportation and that the children were approaching teenage years and would have higher expenses.

C. Deviation from the guidelines

Doe v. Doe, No. 2020-CA-00853-COA, 2021 WL 5193082 (Miss. Ct. App. Nov. 9, 2021).

The court of appeals held that a chancellor abused her discretion in applying the child support guidelines rather than deviating downward based on the noncustodial father's extensive visitation. The couple agreed that the mother would have physical custody and the father would have visitation thirteen days a month (42% of the time). The child support statute provides that a court may deviate based on a parenting arrangement "where the noncustodial parent spends a great deal of time with the children thereby reducing the financial expenditures of the custodial parent." The court of appeals noted that a downward deviation would not harm the children – the wife's income was double that of her husband's. The court remanded, instructing the chancellor to set a "reasonably lower" amount of child support.

D. Add-ons to basic child support

1. Health insurance and medical expenses

Savell v. Manning, 325 So. 3d 1208 (Miss. Ct. App. 2021) The court of appeals reversed and remanded a chancellor's child support order, instructing the court to address health insurance and payment of uncovered medical expenses. At trial, the father's attorney stated that the child was covered by Medicaid and CHIP; however, the chancellor did not address health insurance or medical expenses in the judgment. MISS. CODE ANN. δ 43-19-101(6) states that chancellors "shall" make findings of fact regarding the availability and cost of health insurance. If coverage is not available at a reasonable cost for the parents, the chancellor is to make specific findings to that effect and "make appropriate provisions in the judgment for the payment of medical expenses of the child(ren)." If the court requires the custodial parent to obtain health insurance, its cost shall be taken into account in establishing the child support award. The court of appeals remanded for the chancellor to comply with the mandatory requirement for addressing health insurance. The court noted that if the child was covered by Medicaid or CHIP, the chancellor could order the parties to maintain coverage for so long as the child is eligible.

2. Extracurricular activities

Savell v. Manning, 325 So. 3d 1208 (Miss. Ct. App. 2021). The court of appeals remanded a chancellor's order for payment of extracurricular activities, finding that the order was unclear. The chancellor ordered that the parents share the cost of extracurricular activities in proportion to their incomes. However, no evidence was provided at trial regarding the mother's income. And, it was not clear whether the division was to be based on the parents' current income or to fluctuate as their income fluctuated. The court reversed for the chancellor to state a specific percentage of the costs that each parent would bear.

Smith v. Smith, 318 So. 3d 484 (Miss. Ct. App. 2021). A chancellor properly modified an agreement with regard to extracurricular activities because it was unworkable. The father agreed to pay 100% of activities "mutually agreed upon by the parties in advance." The parents agreed on two activities for their daughter – dance and horseback riding – but disagreed about the amount of the expense. The chancellor eliminated the requirement that the parents agree on activities and modified the father's obligation to a maximum of $6,000 a year per child. The court of appeals affirmed, based on the chancellor's finding that the provision was unworkable because the parents could not agree on activities.

E. Cost of visitation

Jefferson v. Jefferson, 327 So. 3d 1085 (Miss. Ct. App. 2021). A couple agreed at divorce that if one of the parents lived overseas, their son would visit with that parent for the full summer. The chancellor ordered that the father, who intended to live in Japan, would be responsible for all costs of transportation for the summer visit. The court of appeals rejected his argument that transportation costs should be deducted from child support. Chancellors have discretion to divide or allocate visitation costs to one parent. It is error to assign all costs to a noncustodial parent if the expense affects their ability to visit the child. In this case, however, the father testified that he was able to bear the cost while the mother testified that she was not.

F. Tax deductions

Thornton v. Thornton, 322 So. 3d 485 (Miss. Ct. App. 2021). A chancellor who modified custody of one child to the father did not err in awarding the father the tax exemption for that child.

The deduction was more valuable to the working father than to the mother, who was on disability. In addition, the father would now bear more of the costs for the younger son. The court also noted that chancellors are not required to make findings of fact to support assignment of tax exemptions.

G. Modification

1. While child is in boarding school

Smith v. Smith, 318 So. 3d 484 (Miss. Ct. App. 2021). The court of appeals rejected a father's argument that his support obligation for his son should be suspended while the son attended boarding school. The son lived with the noncustodial father for eight months pursuant to an informal agreement between the parents. He then attended the McCallie Preparatory School in Chattanooga for a year before returning to live with his father. At that point custody was formally modified to the father. The chancellor held that the father was in arrears because he did not pay the custodial mother basic support for the boy during the months that he was in boarding school. The father argued that he provided the primary home for his son before and after the period in which the boy was in boarding school and should not be required to pay support to the mother. The court of appeals affirmed the chancellor's order, holding that a parent may not suspend support simply because a child is away at boarding school.

2. Reasonableness of custodial parent's choices

Smith v. Smith, 318 So. 3d 484 (Miss. Ct. App. 2021). The court of appeals rejected a father's argument that the custodial mother's choice of private schools was unreasonable and the cost excessive. At divorce, the father agreed to pay $1,000 a month in support for each child, one-half of the children's tuition at their current private school and "any other such schools they may attend." Two years later, their daughter was diagnosed with dyslexia and Expressive/Receptive Language disorder. The parents agreed that the mother would move to Memphis so that the girl could attend a school for children with dyslexia. Eighteen months later, the mother unilaterally decided to enroll the daughter in the Currey-Ingram School in Nashville, a move that the father objected to as unnecessary, disruptive to his relationship with his daughter, and too expensive. The chancellor ordered that the father pay one-half of the more expensive Currey Ingram tuition, based on his agreement to pay one-half of the costs of any private school that the children "may later attend."

On appeal, the father cited cases stating that a custodial parent's choices regarding education and medical treatment must be reasonable, particularly when they impact a noncustodial parent's financial obligation. The court of appeals acknowledged the requirement of reasonableness but found no abuse of discretion. The mother did provide evidence that Currey Ingram offered advantages not available in the Memphis school. In addition, the father did not prove a material change in circumstances that would warrant reducing his support. The court noted that the divorce agreement did not cap or otherwise limit the costs of private schools.

3. Retroactivity

* *Lacoste v. Lacoste*, 313 So. 3d 1097 (Miss. Ct. App. 2021). The court of appeals rejected a father's argument that the Mississippi child support statute prohibiting retroactive reduction of child support is an unconstitutional taking of property. He did not cite authority for his proposition that courts can make retroactive modifications to accomplish equity in compelling circumstances. The court of appeals reiterated that chancellors have no authority to make reductions in support retroactive. The court also noted that, even if they did, equity was not on the father's side – he filed four requests for continuances, one request for a stay, and a motion to extend trial dates. The court was not to blame for the long delay.

4. Increase in support

*Bennett v. Bennett, 316 So. 3d 651 (Miss. Ct. App. 2021). The court of appeals affirmed a chancellor's modification of a father's child support from $375 a month to $575 a month. The retired father had increased his income by working part-time. Both children wore contacts and needed braces, as well as having increased expenses as a result of being older. The mother also testified that her share of their expenses was greater because the father had not exercised visitation in the last six months.

5. Decrease in support

(a) Based on custody modification

Braswell v. Braswell, 336 So. 3d 1121 (Miss. Ct. App. 2021). A chancellor erred in denying a father's motion to reduce child support. The boy came to live with the noncustodial father five months prior to the court hearing. The father sought modification of his child support and alimony obligations. The chancellor declined to modify either and found that the father was in arrears. The court appeals held that the chancellor erred in refusing to modify the alimony obligation, finding that the father had suffered an involuntary loss of income. In addition, the court held that the chancellor should have terminated the father's child support obligation because the boy now lived with his father. The court also held that the father should not have been charged with arrearages for the five months in which the boy lived with him prior to the modification action.

(b) Denied: No change in standard of living

Stephens v. Stephens, 328 So. 3d 760 (Miss. Ct. App. 2021). A chancellor properly denied a father's request for a reduction in child support. In the couple's 2016 divorce, the father agreed to pay $2,500 a month in child support, provide life insurance, and pay one-half of uncovered medical expenses. The court of appeals agreed with the chancellor's finding that no material change in circumstances had occurred. The father's income had decreased only slightly from the time of divorce, from a gross income of $3,900 a month to $3,686 a month. He had not changed his standard of living and enjoyed luxuries such as overseas travel, concerts, football games, dining out with guests, and going to bars. The fact that the father agreed to pay $2,500 because he expected a pay increase that did not materialize was not a material change in circumstances.

H. Termination of support

Davis v. Henderson, 332 So. 3d 837 (Miss. 2022). The supreme court reversed a court of appeals decision, reinstating a chancellor's order terminating a father's child support obligation. The parents had been involved in extensive litigation over fourteen years when the father filed his sixth contempt petition as well as a petition to terminate support for his teenaged son. The son had refused to visit his father for three years. The chancellor found that the primary reason for the estrangement was the son's desire not to see his father and that the son's conduct was "clear and extreme." The chancellor suspended support temporarily for the family to attend reunification counseling. A year later, the son testified that he still had not visited his father, did not respond to his text messages or calls, and did not want a relationship with him. The court found that the son's continued hostility warranted suspending support until he resumed regular visitation with his father.

The court of appeals reversed, finding that the father's conduct was the primary reason for the estrangement – he was involved in a physically abusive incident four years earlier when he forced his son to hold his hands over his head for so long that he cried. He did not attend the son's band concerts or events or show an interest in his plans. He would not allow his son to use the internet at his house, go outside, or cook at his house.

The supreme court reversed, holding that the court of appeals failed to apply the abuse of discretion standard to review the chancellor's finding that the son's conduct caused the estrangement. Instead, the court of appeals made its own finding that the father's actions were responsible. An appellate court must affirm if there is substantial evidence to support a chancellor's findings. Two justices dissented, arguing that the evidence relied on by the chancellor fell far short of previous cases in which child support was terminated. Those cases involved children who accused parents of rape, filed petitions to terminate their parenthood, or wished them dead. The son in this case participated in court-ordered counseling, said that he loved his father but did not want to visit him, and brainstormed about ways to improve the relationship. His attitude toward his father may have stemmed in part from the years of litigation between his parents and his father's attempt to cut off support.

VIII. ENFORCEMENT

A. Property division

Brown v. Brown, 329 So. 3d 544 (Miss. Ct. App. 2021). A chancellor properly refused to hold a husband in contempt for noncompliance with a couple's property settlement agreement based on the doctrine of clean hands. The couple's irreconcilable differences divorce settlement agreement provided that, within thirty days of the divorce judgment, they would list remaining personal property items and divide those they could agree upon. For items they could not agree upon, they would seek the court's assistance within sixty days of the judgment. Seven months after the judgment, the wife filed a contempt petition alleging that her former husband refused to divide their personal property. At the contempt hearing on November 8, the parties announced in open court that they had agreed to divide the marital property items through a coin toss and alternating selections on the list. The court entered an order on requiring the parties to proceed immediately with the division and to submit proof by November 15 of any items they claimed should be omitted as separate property. The parties met on November 15 to divide the items. However, the wife first demanded that she receive a set of blue dishes. When the husband insisted on following the coin-toss procedure, she walked out. Upon learning of the failed division, the court gave the parties until December 10 to divide the personal property. On December 21, the court entered an order declining to address the personal property issues. The wife filed a second contempt motion seeking to require the husband to participate in the coin-toss division and asking the court to address items alleged to be separate property.

The court of appeals held that the couple's agreement to a coin toss division, dictated into the record at the first contempt hearing, was a binding and enforceable agreement. The wife breached the agreement when she walked out of the meeting at which the coin toss division was to occur. The chancellor did not err in finding that she failed to enforce the agreement and must bear the consequences.

Siders v. Zickler, 312 So. 3d 1224 (Miss. Ct. App. 2021). The court of appeals rejected a husband's argument that he was not obligated to provide a life insurance policy with his wife as beneficiary. Their property settlement agreement stated that he would "continue to maintain the life insurance policy that is now in effect" with his wife as beneficiary. His wife learned ten years after their divorce that the policy had lapsed and her former husband had replaced the policy with a new one with his children and current wife as beneficiaries. When she objected, the husband put her on the policy as beneficiary. However, he let the policy lapse just a few months later. Six years later, she learned of the second lapse and filed a contempt petition based on his failure to maintain insurance. The chancellor found him in contempt and ordered the husband to obtain a new policy with the same face value as the pre-divorce policy. The husband argued that he allowed his insurance policy to lapse BEFORE the property settlement agreement was signed. Thus, he had no obligation under the insurance provision, which required him to maintain the policy "now in effect." The court of appeals noted that when an agreement is not clear, it must be harmonized with the parties' intent. It was clear that the parties referred to a specific policy of insurance – there was only one policy to which they could have referred. By signing the agreement, the husband represented to the court and his wife that the policy was still in effect. Nor did the court err in ordering him to make his wife the owner of the policy so that she would receive notice if it was cancelled. His failure to comply with the agreement necessitated the court's order making her the owner.

B. Contempt

1. Willfulness

Stephens v. Stephens, 328 So. 3d 760 (Miss. Ct. App. 2021). A chancellor did not err in finding a father in contempt for nonpayment of child support, even though he was unemployed for part of the period in which arrearages accrued. He voluntarily left his job when he faced incarceration for nonpayment of child support, so that he would not be fired. However, at that point he had two months to satisfy the arrearages.

2. Failure to pay not willful

Braswell v. Braswell, 336 So. 3d 1121 (Miss. Ct. App. 2021). The court of appeals reversed a chancellor's finding of contempt, holding that the father proved that he was unable to pay $7,000 a month in child support and alimony. He lost income when he entered inpatient treatment for substance abuse, was required to work limited hours, and had to close his office during Covid. He attempted to find other work, paid only those bills necessary to keep his practice open, depleted his assets, and lived frugally. In addition, he promptly filed a petition for modification when his office was closed in 2018. While he remained liable for arrearages, he should not have been found in contempt.

3. Technical violation

Savell v. Manning, 325 So. 3d 1208 (Miss. Ct. App. 2021). A chancellor properly refused to find a father in contempt for violating the terms of supervised weekend visitations. He was alone with his son on several occasions for five minutes when he drove from one supervisor's home to another and he was briefly alone with his son while a supervisor was in another room. The purpose of the order was to require weekend visitation in a supervisor's home, not that the supervisor watch the father and child at all times.

4. For withholding visitation

Thornton v. Thornton, 322 So. 3d 485 (Miss. Ct. App. 2021). A chancellor did not err in finding a mother in contempt for violating a visitation schedule and failure to comply with her obligations as a joint legal custodian. She listed her boyfriend as an emergency contact instead of the father. She did not inform the father of the boy's failing grades, medical problems, or let him know about events. She enrolled the boy in a different school without telling the father. She refused to allow him visitation if he was delayed by work. The chancellor was not required to hold the father in contempt for trespass on the mother's home when he was confused about the time of visitation.

C. Defenses to enforcement

1. Disagreement with court orders

Savell v. Manning, 325 So. 3d 1208 (Miss. Ct. App. 2021). The court of appeals affirmed a chancellor's finding that a mother was in civil and criminal contempt for violating court-ordered visitation provisions at least fourteen times. The mother admitted that she repeatedly refused to allow her son to have court-ordered visitation, stating that she was trying to protect him. It is not a defense to contempt that a parent believes the court's order to be wrong.

2. Statute of limitations

*Siders v. Zickler, 312 So. 3d 1224 (Miss. Ct. App. 2021). A wife's contempt action was not barred by the statute of limitations. In their 2002 divorce, her ex-husband agreed to maintain a life insurance policy. The policy was cancelled in November 2013. The wife filed her petition for contempt in 2019. The husband argued that the three-year statute of limitations on contracts applied. The court held that because a property settlement agreement is incorporated into a judgment, the seven-year statute of limitations on enforcing judgments applies.

*Coleman v. WGST, LLC, 328 So. 3d 698 (Miss. Ct. App. 2021). A chancellor properly dismissed an ex-wife's action to set aside a deed based on the running of the statute of limitations. The couple divorced in 2010 in Tennessee. In 2012, the wife enrolled the Tennessee judgment in DeSoto County. The hus-

band conveyed property to WGST in 2015. The wife filed suit on July 9, 2019, seeking to set aside the deed and enforce the lien. The court of appeals agreed with the chancellor that the action was governed by Miss. Code Ann. §§ 11-7-303 and 15-1-45, which state that the statute of limitations on a foreign judgment runs seven years after rendition of the judgment. The court rejected the wife's argument that the seven-year statute began to run when she enrolled the judgment, rather than from the rendition of the judgment. The court also rejected her argument that Miss. Code Ann. § 15-1-43, which allows renewal of a judgment, applied to the case. By its terms, the statute applies only to domestic judgments.

D. Incarceration for criminal contempt

Savell v. Manning, 325 So. 3d 1208 (Miss. Ct. App. 2021). A chancellor properly ordered a mother incarcerated for thirty days as punishment for criminal contempt and suspended the sentence contingent on her compliance with visitation orders. The court rejected the mother's argument that the chancellor's suspended jail sentence, conditioned on compliance with visitation, was an order of probation until the child was twenty-one. She argued that the order violated the statutory five-year limit on probation. Probation, which requires monitoring and reporting to an officer, is not the same thing as a suspended sentence. A chancellor has authority to suspend a jail sentence conditioned on compliance with an order. The court did note that under Miss. Code Ann. § 99-19-25, circuit courts and county courts cannot revoke a suspended sentence in misdemeanor cases after five years. The court declined to address whether the statute applied to chancery courts or to sentences based on contempt but noted that the mother could raise the issue if revocation occurred beyond five year.

IX. Paternity

A. Statute of limitations

Friday v. Mississippi Dep't Human Servs., 325 So. 3d 1200 (Miss. Ct. App. 2021). A chancery court had jurisdiction over a paternity and support action even though the child turned twenty-one while the proceedings were pending. The relevant statute provides that a paternity suit must be instituted, not completed, before a child is twenty-one years of age. The chancellor properly took jurisdiction when the boy was twenty years of age and ordered the father to pay one year of back support in the amount of $200 a month. The defendant's refusal to submit to court-ordered genetic testing raised a presumption of paternity that he did not rebut. DHS was not required to provide proof that the boy was unemancipated when the suit was filed. The burden of proof is on a parent claiming emancipation as a defense to support.

B. Presumption of paternity: Inheritance

Randle v. Randle, No. 2020-CA-00433-COA, 2021 WL 4972443 (Miss. Ct. App. Oct. 26, 2021). An estate administrator rebutted the presumption that a deceased was the biological father of two children by his first marriage. The presumed father died intestate, survived by his second wife and their son and two children of his first marriage. In addition, a woman claimed that she was the deceased's nonmarital child. The chancellor ordered DNA testing of all four persons claiming to be his children. The results showed that the child of his second marriage and the woman claiming to be a nonmarital child were half-siblings. However, the results showed a high probability that the children of his first marriage were not related to either of the half-siblings. The deceased's widow testified that her husband had sought legal advice about disestablishing his paternity of the claimants but was told that he could not because he had been married to their mother. The chancellor denied the claimants' request to exhume the body for DNA testing but ruled that they could do so at their expense.

The court of appeals rejected the claimants' argument that the administrator/wife was barred from contesting their paternity based on the clean hands doctrine. In fact, as administrator, it was her duty to do so. The court agreed with the claimants that they were presumed to be the children of their mother's husband but held that the administrator rebutted the presumption with DNA evidence regarding the relationship between the half-siblings and the claimants. The court was not required to exhume the deceased's body to obtain DNA evidence.

C. Presumption of paternity: Genetic testing

Greer v. Greer, 312 So. 3d 414 (Miss. Ct. App. 2021). The court of appeals affirmed a chancellor's order finding that a husband was the father of his wife's child conceived during their separation and reconciliation attempts. The husband filed a motion in divorce proceedings seeking a determination of the child's paternity. The court ordered genetic testing within thirty days. At the time of trial a year later, the husband had not submitted to testing. He did not appear at the trial. The chancellor held that the child was born of the marriage and ordered the husband to pay child support. The court of appeals affirmed. Under the Mississippi paternity statutes, a husband may contest his legal fatherhood of a child born during the marriage. The chancellor must order genetic tests and may resolve the issue of paternity against one who refuses to submit to the test. The chancellor properly resolved the issue of paternity against the husband, finding him to be the child's legal father.

X.   YOUTH COURT PROCEEDINGS

A. Durable legal custody

In re Interest of M.M., 319 So. 3d 1188 (Miss. Ct. App. 2021). The court of appeals affirmed a youth court's award of durable legal custody of three children to their maternal grandfather, after the father failed to comply with the CPS reunification plan and drug court recommendations. The children were taken from their father's home after a report that the house was uninhabitable and that the children lacked access to adequate food and water to bathe. The children were adjudicated neglected and placed with their grandfather. The father agreed to correct deficiencies in the home, submit to drug testing, enroll in counseling, and participate in the family drug court program. The drug court staff, the youth court judge, and DCPS recommended that he enter a treatment program for overuse of fentanyl and that he pursue surgical options for pain relief. He insisted that he did not need treatment. After six months, DCPS and the children's attorney recommended changing the plan from reunification to permanent placement in durable legal custody. The children were placed with their grandfather. The court of appeals rejected the father's argument that DCPS did not make clear to him that a failure to enter treatment would result in a loss of his children. The court also rejected his argument that the court should have considered placing the children with one of his relatives. Durable legal custody may only be awarded to a person who has had physical custody of the children for six months under DCPS oversight. The court also rejected his argument that the trial court should have engaged in an *Albright* analysis, which is not required when a court finds that a parent is unfit to have custody. In addition, he did not appeal the adjudication order in which the children were first placed with the grandfather.

B. Youth court procedure and notice of rights

In re Interest of M.M., 319 So. 3d 1188 (Miss. Ct. App. 2021). The court of appeals rejected a father's argument that a youth court erred by failing to advise him of his rights, including the right to appeal, as required by Miss. CODE ANN. δ 43-21-557(1)(e) ("At the beginning of each adjudicatory hearing, the youth court shall explain to the parties . . . the right to appeal). The failure was harmless error – the father was represented by counsel at the adjudication hearing and the disposition hearing. His attorney participated in the hearings and made no complaint about the failure to advise his client.

M.A.S. v. Lamar County CPS, No. 2020-CA-00070-COA, 2021 WL 4271909 (Miss. Ct. App. Sept. 21, 2021). The court of appeals rejected a mother's argument that termination of her parental rights should be reversed because the youth court failed to provide notice of her rights at the adjudicatory hearing, failed to hold a separate disposition hearing, and did not advise her of her rights in the termination hearing until late in the proceedings. She also argued that the petition to adjudicate the children as neglected was insufficient to inform her of the basis for the petition.

The court of appeals held that she waived arguments related to the adjudication and disposition hearings because she did not appeal from those orders. In addition, she waived arguments related to notice at the adjudication hearing and to the failure to hold a separate disposition hearing because she was represented by counsel at both hearings and made no objection. The court also held that failure to comply with the statutory notice requirements does not automatically require reversal. Because she was represented by counsel, the failure was harmless error at best.

The mother also argued that the youth court failed to advise her of her rights at the termination hearing at which she appeared *pro se*, waiting until several witnesses had been heard and evidence introduced. The court of appeals held that the youth court substantially complied with the requirements by providing notice during the proceedings. The mother showed no prejudice as a result of the delay.

XI. TERMINATION OF PARENTAL RIGHTS

A. Physical abuse

Coulter v. Dunn, 312 So. 3d 713 (Miss. 2021). The supreme court affirmed a chancellors' termination of a mother's parental rights. Child Protective Services took custody when the nine-week-old child was admitted to the hospital with a broken femur. The treating physician, also a child abuse specialist, testified that in two months the child had suffered multiple severe injuries that could only have been caused by abuse, including rib fractures, hip fracture, fractures above and below both knees, and ankle fractures. The child lived with her paternal grandparents for four years, with the mother having supervised visitation. After four years, the grandparents sought to adopt her. The chancellor found that the mother was responsible for her child's injuries, based on testimony that she was the only person with custody during the time in which the injuries occurred. The court of appeals affirmed – a court may infer that parents are responsible for abuse when they are the only persons with custody of a child.

B. Substance abuse

M.A.S. v. Lamar County CPS, No. 2020-CA-00070-COA, 2021 WL 4271909 (Miss. Ct. App. Sept. 21, 2021). The court of appeals affirmed a chancellor's termination of a mother's parental rights. Her three children were taken from her home in response to reports of the mother's drug abuse and excessive school absences by the children. The reunification plan required that she take bi-monthly drug tests and that she visit with the children and become involved in their education. The children were returned to her for ninety days but removed again when she tested positive for drugs. Over the next six months, she refused to take drug tests and did not exercise visitation with the children. She did not attend family team meetings or respond to CPS calls. The court held that CPS should discontinue reunification efforts and work toward adoption. Evidence at the termination hearing showed that two of the three children were born with drugs in their bodies, that the mother refused most drug tests, attempted to secure her own tests with a relative's urine, and tested positive when she was tested properly. She did not visit the children regularly, resulting in an erosion of the parent-child relationship. The chancellor found that the mother's rights should be terminated based on a habitual drug addiction that she was unable to control and that contributed to a substantial erosion of the parent-child relationship.

C. No contact with child

Smith v. Doe, 314 So. 3d 154 (Miss. Ct. App. 2021). A chancellor properly terminated the rights of a father who had not seen his seven-year-old son for five years, finding that the father had abandoned his son and that there was a substantial erosion of the parent-child relationship. The boy had been raised by his stepfather, who wanted to adopt him, and who the boy viewed as his father. The court of appeals rejected the father's argument that he had not abandoned his son because he paid child support. The court also held that the boy's mother did not prevent him from seeing his son. He attempted unsuccessfully to work out a visitation plan with her outside of court. When the boy was one, she brought him to meet the father at a restaurant but refused to allow him to visit at his apartment. The father visited with the boy at a hotel nine months later when the child was almost two. Over the next five years, his only contact was to send Christmas presents in 2014. The gifts were returned. The father testified that he instructed his child support attorney to seek visitation, but the attorney delayed for two years. His attorney then withdrew, resulting in a delay of another year. The guardian ad litem recommended termination based on the father's failure to visit with the boy in five years, resulting in a complete lack of a relationship between the two. The court of appeals affirmed. Abandonment may be proved by showing that on the date of the petition, the parent has deliberately made no contact with a child over the age of three for one year. The court did not accept the father's argument that the mother kept him from seeing his son or that, for five years, he relied on his attorneys to obtain visitation. He could have contacted the mother about visitation even though litigation was pending. In fact, she invited him to the boy's fifth birthday party, which he did not attend because of work. The court stated that "a mistaken belief that a parent was not allowed to contact another parent pending a termination of parental rights suit does not overcome a clear and convincing showing of abandonment."

XII.   ADOPTION

*Adoption of A.M., 323 So. 3d 509 (Miss. 2021). The supreme court affirmed a chancellor's order withdrawing acceptance of a mother's consent to adoption. The unmarried mother, who became unemployed shortly after her child's birth, signed a consent to adoption on July 27, 2019. On July 30, the chancellor entered a temporary order finding that the surrender form "complied with applicable statutes and is accepted by the Court" and allowing the adoptive mother to take the child to Georgia. On August 26, the biological mother filed a withdrawal of consent. The case was delayed because of difficulty in serving the biological father. After a hearing on January 30, 2020, the court entered an order finding that she should not have stated in her temporary order that the consent was accepted because no hearing had been held. The chancellor allowed the mother to withdraw her consent to adoption, stating her belief that the mother signed the consent under financial and economic duress. The supreme court rejected the adopting mother's argument that the consent could not be withdrawn. Prior to 2016, a parent's consent to adoption was final when they signed a con-

sent form, absent proof of duress. Under the new Termination of Parental Rights Law, Miss. Code Ann. δ 93-15-107(2), a court's order "accepting the parent's written voluntary release terminates all of the parent's parental rights." Under the new statute, termination does not occur until a court accepts the surrender. The supreme court held that the chancellor effectively rescinded her acceptance of the consent, and the mother withdrew it prior to acceptance. One justice disagreed with the majority that the chancellor did not accept the surrender. However, the justice agreed with the result because a chancellor has discretion to modify or reverse an interlocutory order for any reason it deems sufficient.

XIII. GUARDIANSHIPS AND CONSERVATORSHIPS

In re Conservatorship of Walls, 322 So. 3d 474 (Miss. Ct. App. 2021). A chancellor did not err in appointing a man's sister, rather than his wife, as his conservator. The court rejected the wife's argument that the sister had a conflict of interest because, at the time she was appointed temporary conservator, she was under indictment for exploiting her brother. The complaint was filed by the man's daughter who was concerned about a $10,000 transfer from her father to her aunt. The daughter withdrew her complaint when she learned that the transfer was to repay his sister for a loan she made to prevent foreclosure of his property. The court noted that there is no preference for a spouse to be appointed conservator of a person. The husband and wife had been estranged for twenty years prior to his illness. While serving as a temporary conservator, she was in contempt for fifteen months for failure to provide the court with expenses and for preventing the husband's family from visiting him.

XIV. PROCEDURE

A. Service of process

Johnson v. Smith, No. 2019-CA-01450-COA, 2021 WL1381090 (Miss. Ct. App. April 13, 2021). The court of appeals affirmed a chancellor's order granting parents joint legal and physical custody for eleven months until their child started school and then continuing joint legal custody, with the father having physical custody. The court rejected the mother's argument that the judgment was void because she was not properly served with a Rule 81 summons for a continued hearing. The hearing was continued from the original date but was not rescheduled until later. The court agreed that the mother should have been served with a new Rule 81 summons. However, she waived the objection by appearing and participating in the action. She did not raise the issue until after the trial was completed.

B. Motions to recuse

Lockhart v. Lockhart, 324 So. 3d 777 (Miss. 2021). A chancellor properly denied a husband's motion that she recuse herself because his wife's lawyer's firm hosted a fundraiser for the judge and because the judge once worked for the law firm. The wife's attorney was not a major contributor to the judge's campaign. And, it had been over fifteen years since the judge worked for the founder of the firm.

Thornton v. Thornton, 322 So. 3d 485 (Miss. Ct. App. 2021). The court of appeals rejected a wife's argument that a chancellor should have recused himself after she posted on a Go Fund Me account that she "was being treated unfairly by a biased judge" in a custody modification action. She argued that the Go Fund Me page, which the husband presented as evidence of contempt, would bias the judge against her. The judge refused, stating that the post would not influence his decision. The court of appeals agreed that the wife failed to produce evidence to overcome the presumption that a judge is unbiased.

C. Trials

1. Right to trial

*Kreps v. Hyland, 331 So. 3d 590 (Miss. Ct. App. 2021). A mother's due process rights were denied when a custody hearing was continued in her absence. She was arrested for having a suspended license and sent to jail while she was waiting in the courthouse for the trial to begin. She was released to attend the trial later in the day. By that time, four witnesses had testified for the father. The chancellor excluded her three witnesses because they had been in the courtroom when the judge invoked Rule 615 and did not identify themselves. The chancellor awarded the father custody of their daughter, who was delivered to the courthouse to go with the father to Louisiana. The mother was returned to jail. The court of appeals emphasized that a parent's liberty interest in the care and custody of their children is protected by the Due Process Clause and is "perhaps one of the oldest of the fundamental liberty interests." Procedural due process includes the right to a fair trial, to be present and to be heard, to offer evidence, and to call and cross-examine witnesses. There was no persuasive reason to continue without the mother. She was present for the trial and her arrest was unrelated to the proceeding. Continuing in her absence deprived her of an opportunity to cross-examine her husband's witnesses and to present her own witnesses. The court also cited cases discussing the importance of hearing from both parents in child custody cases.

2. Judicial notice

Doe v. Doe, No. 2020-CA-00853-COA, 2021 WL 5193082 (Miss. Ct. App. Nov. 9, 2021). A chancellor erred in finding that a husband infected his wife with a sexually transmitted disease. The wife tested positive for herpes and genital warts caused by the HPV virus shortly after the couple separated. The husband tested negative for herpes in three separate tests. He testified that he had never had genital warts, for which there is no test in the absence of symptoms. The wife's expert physician stated that it was likely that she contracted HPV from her husband if (as she stated) she was monogamous and because her pap smears were always normal. She did not inform her doctor that she had abnormal pap smears in the past and had been treated fifteen years earlier for an HPV-related condition, cervical dysplasia. The chancellor took judicial notice of the fact that there are hundreds of strains of HPV, some which cause dysplasia and some that cause genital warts. The chancellor found that the husband presented no evidence that the 2003 infection and the current infection were linked and found it reasonable to infer that the wife contracted the infection from her husband.

The court of appeals held that the chancellor's use of judicial notice was error. A court may take judicial notice of matters commonly known in the community or which "can be accurately and readily determined from sources whose accuracy cannot reasonably be questioned" such as maps, tables, census data, or dates and times. Whether a particular strain of HPV can cause a disease and whether the two infections were related were matters requiring testimony from a medical expert.

3. Evidence

Kerr v. Kerr, 323 So. 3d 462 (Miss. 2021). The supreme court rejected a mother's argument that her son's medical records were hearsay and should have been excluded from evidence. The records qualified under the business records exception to hearsay. It was made by someone with knowledge, in a record kept in the course of a regular business activity. The manager of the medical clinic provided an affidavit that the record was a true and correct copy.

Myers v. Myers, 324 So. 3d 808 (Miss. Ct. App. 2021). A chancellor properly allowed a father unsupervised visitation with his daughters, finding no evidence to support the mother's repeated allegations that he had sexually abused one of the girls. Nor did the court err in refusing to admit a letter from the son's counselor as inadmissible hearsay. She offered the letter to prove abuse based on the counselor's report of a statement by their son. Similarly, the court properly excluded the mother's recording of one of their daughters saying that she did not want to visit her father because he hurt her. The recording contained hearsay that did not fall under either the present sense impression or excited utterance exception. The incident to which she allegedly referred in the recording had occurred two years earlier.

4. Attorney-client privilege

Pace v. Pace, 324 So. 3d 369 (Miss. Ct. App. 2021). A wife did not waive the attorney-client privilege with regard to emails between her and her attorney by a brief reference to an email between them. The wife merely mentioned the email in explaining how she arrived at the amount of cash she claimed to have in her possession.

D. Post-trial motions

1. Motion for findings

* *Roley v. Roley,* 329 So. 3d 473 (Miss. Ct. App. 2021). The court of appeals rejected a husband's argument that the chancellor should have made requested findings of fact and conclusions of law on the husband's post-trial motion for reconsideration. A court is required to provide findings of fact upon request after a trial. However, courts have discretion whether to provide findings of fact on post-trial matters.

2. Motion to set aside judgment for fraud on the court

Thornton v. Thornton, 322 So. 3d 485 (Miss. Ct. App. 2021). A chancellor erred in finding that a mother's post-trial motion was untimely. At the first trial of this matter, the chancellor awarded the wife a truck, relying on the husband's 8.05 financial statement indicating the truck had an outstanding loan balance of $4,000. The amount was actually $9,862. While his wife's appeal of the judgment was pending, she filed a timely Rule 60(b) motion alleging fraud on the court based on his misrepresentation of the loan balance. After the case was remanded two years later, the wife filed an amended Rule 60(b) motion alleging that the husband also committed fraud on the court by using the truck as collateral for a $2,000 loan after the divorce hearing. The chancellor held that the amended motion was untimely because it was not filed within sixty days of the judgment. The court of appeals reversed. A motion to set aside based on fraud on the court is not limited by the sixty-day time period but must be filed within a reasonable time. The court remanded for the chancellor to consider the proffered testimony on the amended motion to set aside.

3. Clarification of unclear order

Lockhart v. Lockhart, 324 So. 3d 777 (Miss. 2021). A chancellor did not err in clarifying a year-old property division judgment by providing a means for enforcing the order and by specifying values for the properties involved. The chancellor's 2018 order divided assets between spouses, including the marital home, rental properties, post-separation income from their businesses, and vehicles. The order provided that the marital home and one rental property should be sold, and the proceeds divided equally, that the wife would be entitled to one-half of the equity in two parcels held by the husband and the husband entitled to one-half of the equity in two properties held by the wife, and that each was entitled to one-half of the proceeds earned by the other in their respective businesses through August 2017. The order was not appealed. A year later, the wife petitioned for contempt, arguing that the husband failed to relinquish property awarded to her. He countered with a petition for contempt based on her failure to cooperate with the sale of the marital home. A special master appointed by the chancellor recommended that all the properties be valued and sold. The chancellor entered an order clarifying the 2018 order, noting that while she had no authority to modify property division, the order was vague and needed clarification. In particular, the order did not establish the equity in the properties. The court looked to the testimony presented at trial to determine the value and debt for each property, ordering the owning spouse to pay one-half of the resulting equity to the other. The court clarified that "profits" meant gross profits minus cost of goods. The chancellor calculated the amount owed by the husband, offset the amount that his wife owed, and ordered that he pay her $53,992.50 within thirty days of the order.

The husband arguing that by assigning values to the properties and ordering payment, the court improperly modified the 2018 property division. The supreme court disagreed. The court's assignment of values and order for payment provided a self-effectuating method of enforcing the order, which both parties had failed to comply with. It did not alter the award but clarified it after both parties complained that the order was ambiguous.

E. Appeals

1. Time period for notice of appeal

In re Interest of M.M., 319 So. 3d 1188 (Miss. Ct. App. 2021). A father's request to extend the time for appeal was untimely. He appealed a December 28, 2017 adjudication order and June 25, 2018 permanency order on August 13, 2018. On October 31, 2018, he petitioned the trial court to accept his notice of appeal out of time because he failed to meet the thirty-day time period for appeal. The court of appeals held that a court may only extend the time period for filing a notice of appeal for up to 180 days. His request was made more than 180 days after the time period.

Rahman v. Lyons, 332 So. 3d 311 (Miss. Ct. App. 2021). A husband failed to timely appeal a chancellor's denial of his petition to set aside a property settlement agreement. The appellant husband agreed to pay alimony and maintain life insurance with his appellee husband as beneficiary. Four months later, he petitioned to set the agreement aside, arguing that he signed it under duress and coercion. His spouse filed a separate petition for contempt for nonpayment of alimony. The appellant husband later amended his petition to request that the divorce be set aside because the court lacked jurisdiction. He alleged that neither party was a resident of Mississippi, even though the joint complaint stated that his husband was a Mississippi resident. The chancellor denied the petition to set aside based on lack of jurisdiction on August 26, 2019. On April 29, 2020, the chancellor heard the appellee's husband's motion and entered a contempt judgment. On July 29, 2020, the appellant filed notice to appeal both the denial of his petition to set aside and the order of contempt. The court of appeals held that the notice was not timely to appeal the August 2019 denial of his request to set aside. His husband's contempt petition was a separate action, not a counterclaim, filed many months after the petition to set aside was filed. And, because his argument to set aside the contempt was also based on subject matter jurisdiction, there was no merit to the appeal. Having failed to appeal his allegation of lack of subject matter jurisdiction, the husband could not now attack it collaterally in another appeal.

2. Contempt pending appeal

Stephens v. Stephens, 328 So. 3d 760 (Miss. Ct. App. 2021). The court of appeals rejected a father's argument that a chancellor lacked jurisdiction to hear a contempt petition filed while a child support modification judgment was on appeal. Even if the court's refusal to reduce his support was reversed on appeal, the father's support obligation continued pending the appeal. A reduction in child support is only effective from the date of the modification judgment.

3. Right to appeal *in forma pauperis*

Roley v. Roley, 329 So. 3d 473 (Miss. Ct. App. 2021). The court of appeals rejected a husband's argument that he had a constitutional right to proceed *in forma pauperis* on his appeal of a divorce and custody matter. The court distinguished United States Supreme Court cases holding that indigent parents facing termination of parental rights are constitutionally entitled to appeal *in forma pauperis*. The father was given visitation rights with his children, a significantly different matter from losing all parental rights.

4. Failure to cite authority

Carter v. Carter, 324 So. 3d 327 (Miss. Ct. App. 2021). A pro se father's appeal of a visitation modification was procedurally barred because he cited no authority for his arguments. The court of appeals stated that the appeal consisted of "blanket assertions" that the chancellor erred or that the father was prejudiced. An appellant has the burden of supporting his argument with "reasons and authorities."

XV. ATTORNEYS' FEES

A. Findings of fact

Coleman v. Coleman, 324 So. 3d 1204 (Miss. Ct. App. 2021). The court of appeals rejected a husband's argument that a chancellor erred by failing to consider the *McKee* factors in denying him attorneys' fees. The factors are used to determine the appropriate amount of fees and need not be addressed if the spouse fails to prove inability to pay his fees. Although the husband testified that he had to borrow money to pay his fees, he provided no documentation to support his claim.

Savell v. Manning, 325 So. 3d 1208 (Miss. Ct. App. 2021). The court of appeals affirmed a chancellor's finding that a mother was in civil and criminal contempt for violating court-ordered visitation provisions at least fourteen times. The chancellor properly ordered her to pay the husband's attorneys' fees of $2,400. The chancellor's failure to address the *McKee* factors did not require reversal – there was sufficient evidence in the record to support the award of $800 for each of three contempt hearings necessitated by the mother's conduct.

B. Review with remand of financial awards

Hammond v. Hammond, 327 So. 3d 173 (Miss. Ct. App. 2021). A chancellor did not err in denying a wife's request for attorneys' fees. She was awarded sufficient funds in the property division to pay the outstanding fees of $3,600. However, because the court reversed the chancellor's property division and alimony award, the chancellor could reconsider the attorneys' fees on remand in light of any changes to the awards.

C. Sanctions

Doe v. Doe, No. 2020-CA-00853-COA, 2021 WL 5193082 (Miss. Ct. App. Nov. 9, 2021).

The court of appeals held that a chancellor erred in ordering a husband and his attorney to pay $2,500 each as a sanction for discovery violations. The chancellor found that the husband failed to properly respond to discovery questions and that his filing of over forty subpoenas to his wife's church, doctors, dentist, utility providers, personal trainer, banks and phone service was motivated by ill will and for the purpose of harassment. The court of appeals disagreed that his actions were motivated by ill will, noted that he supplemented his discovery answers and cured any deficiencies, and held that the subpoenas were reasonably filed in order to obtain evidence about the wife's income and expenses. Three judges dissented on this point, arguing that there was sufficient evidence to support the chancellor's sanctions.

D. Guardian ad litem fees

Carter v. Carter, 324 So. 3d 327 (Miss. Ct. App. 2021). A chancellor properly ordered that a pro se father and mother split guardian ad litem fees in an action to modify visitation. The father was the non-prevailing party and the one who requested the hearing.

XVI. TORT ACTIONS

A. Conversion of separate property

Hatton v. Hatton, 323 So. 3d 1149 (Miss. Ct. App. 2021). A chancellor properly declined to address division of a couple's only significant asset, the marital home, based on their prenuptial agreement. The court also held that the chancellor did not err in failing to address the husband's allegation that his wife dissipated his separate property, apparently by pressuring him to use premarital funds to pay her debts. The court of appeals noted that only marital property is subject to equitable distribution. The husband's allegation that his wife converted his separate property "would be a claim for a separate action."

B. Employer liability for husband's actions

Woodard v. Miller, 326 So. 3d 439 (Miss. 2021). The supreme court affirmed a circuit court judge's grant of summary judgment to a religious organization and a minister on a wife's claim that they failed to protect her from contracting HIV from her minister husband. He had multiple affairs with men while he was a minister in the Methodist church. When he told his wife that he was HIV positive, the couple called a Methodist minister and psychotherapist with certification in sex addiction. She met with them the following day for crisis support. She advised the husband to dispose of any electronic pornographic material and to shut down email accounts used to contact partners.

The wife sued the Methodist Conference, alleging that it failed to follow church policy prohibiting homosexuals from serving as ministers. She argued that if the church had been diligent in following its policies, it would have discovered her husband's conduct and warned her, avoiding the injury to her. The supreme court held that states are constitutionally barred from enforcing religious doctrine and may not hold a religious institution to a higher standard based on church doctrine. The church could be held liable, if at all, on rules applicable to any employer. Under Mississippi law, an employer has no duty to uncover an employee's concealed, personal activities. In fact, recent amendments to Title VII would make it illegal for an employer to discriminate on the basis of homosexuality. The court also rejected the wife's argument that the church was vicariously liable. Her husband's affairs were not performed in the course and scope of his church duties and there was no evidence that the church knew of and ratified his behavior.

The court also rejected the wife's argument that her minister friend owed her a fiduciary duty. Being a minister does not in itself give rise to a fiduciary duty – there must be a relationship in which one person is in a position to exercise a dominant influence on the other. The defendant was not the wife's minister, and they were not in a confidential relationship. One day of crisis counseling did not give rise to a fiduciary duty with respect to conduct that occurred prior to the counseling. The court reversed the trial court's denial of summary judgment for the Methodist Conference and Methodist minister.

The supreme court affirmed the trial court's denial of the husband's motion for summary judgment based on the wife's alleged release of claims. The couple's divorce decree stated that "each fully, finally, and forever releases the other from any and all claims, obligations and/or causes of action in this matter." The husband raised the affirmative defense of waiver in his answer to the wife's complaint in the tort action. However, he did not pursue the defense for over two years while he participated in the discovery process. He then joined the Methodist Conference in a motion for summary judgment based on the release in the divorce agreement. The supreme court relied on a 2006 arbitration case, *MS Credit Center, Inc. v. Horton,* 926 So. 2d 167 (Miss. 2006), which states that a "defendant's failure to timely and reasonably raise and pursue the enforcement of any affirmative defense or other affirmative matter or right which would serve to terminate or stay the litigation, coupled with active participation in the litigation process, will ordinarily serve as a waiver." The court held that the husband waived the defense by failing to pursue it within a reasonable time. Two justices dissented, arguing that *Horton* should be limited to waiver based on delay in pursuing the defense of failure to arbitrate. The dissenters argued that waiting to raise the right to arbitration has a greater effect that waiting to raise affirmative defenses such as waiver of claims.

C. Malicious prosecution

Wilbourn v. Wilbourn, 314 So. 3d 104 (Miss. 2021). The Mississippi Supreme Court affirmed a circuit court judge's partial summary judgment to a woman whose former husband sued her for malicious prosecution and intentional and negligent infliction of emotional distress. The mother filed a police report of abuse after a chancellor found that her accusations of sexual misconduct against her husband were unfounded. The matter was referred to a district attorney who initially declined to pursue charges. However, after interviewing the children at the mother's request, the D.A. presented the case to a grand jury which returned a no bill. The husband filed suit against his former wife when he learned of the grand jury proceedings. The supreme court held that the trial judge properly granted the wife summary judgment on the malicious prosecution claim – she did not institute criminal proceedings. A prosecution is commenced by the issuance of a warrant, by indictment, or by affidavit. The husband was not indicted or arrested. His wife's police report statement was not an affidavit commencing criminal proceedings.

BELL FAMILY LAW CLE 2022
UPDATE ON GUARDIAN AND LITEM
AND YOUTH COURT LAW

David L. Calder, University of Miss. Child Advocacy Clinic
phone (662) 915-7394; e-mail: davidcalder23@gmail.com

TABLE OF CONTENTS

I. UPDATE ON GUARDIAN AD LITEM CASES 59
   A. ROLE OF THE GAL AS A LAY WITNESS 59
      1. *Summers v. Gros,* 319 So. 3d 479 (Miss. 2021) 59

   B. CASES RECOGNIZING THE GAL AS AN EXPERT WITNESS 60
      1. Rules 701-706, Miss.R.Evid. 60
      2. *S.G. v. D.C.,* 13 So.3d 269 (Miss. 2009) 61
      3. *D.J.L. v. Bolivar County DHS,* 824 So.2d 617 (Miss. 2002) 61
      4. *McDonald v. McDonald,* 39 So.3d 868 (Miss. 2010) 61
      5. *Ballard v. Ballard,* 255 So.3d 126 (Miss. 2017) 62
      6. *Barber v. Barber,* 288 So.3d 325 (Miss. 2020) 62

   C. LIMITED ROLE FOR THE GAL...63
      1. *Smith v. Smith,* 206 So.3d 502 (Miss. 2016) 63

   D. MANDATORY VS. DISCRETIONARY APPOINTMENT OF GAL 63
      1. *Gibson v. Gibson,* 333 So.3d 103 (Miss. Ct. App. 2022)................63
      2. *Warren v. Rhea,* 318 So. 3d 1187 (Miss. Ct. App. 2021)................64
      3. *Savell v. Manning,* 325 So. 3d 1208 (Miss. Ct. App. 2021).............65
      4. *Embrey v. Young,* ___ So.3d. ___, 2021 WL 5576070 (Miss. Ct.
   App. No. 2021-CA-00091-COA, decided Nov. 30, 2021) 65

   E. REBUTTING THE NATURAL PARENT PRESUMPTION FOR CUSTODY 65
      1. *Roberts v. Conner,* 332 So.3d 272 (Miss. Ct. App. 2021) 65
      2. *Summers v. Gros,* 319 So.3d 479 (Miss. 2021) 66

   F. MODIFICATION OF CUSTODY - - MATERIAL CHANGE IN
   CIRCUMSTANCES STANDARD 68
      1. *Kreppner v. Kreppner,* ___ So.3d ___, 2022 WL 841961 (Miss.
   Ct. App. Decided March 22, 2022) 68
      2. *Carter v. Carter,* 324 So.3d 327 (Miss. Ct. App. 2021) 68

   G. IMPUTING OR ANTICIPATING CHILD ABUSE OR NEGLECT
   BASED ON THE FACTS AND CIRCUMSTANCES 69
      1. *Coulter v. Dunn,* 312 So. 3d 713 (Miss. 2021) 69

2. *Interest of K.M. v. Jackson County Youth Court,* ___ So.3d ___,
2020 WL 7056087 (Miss. Ct. App. decided 12/01/2020) 70
3. *In Interest of N.M. v. Mississippi DHS,* 215 So.3d 1007
(Miss. Ct. App. 2017) 70

H. YOUTH COURT PROCEDURES AND NOTICE OF RIGHTS
AT ADJUDICATION HEARINGS UNDER RULE 24, URYCP 71
1. *Interest of M.M.,* 319 So. 3d 1188 (Miss. Ct. App. 2021) 71
2. *M.A.S. v. Lamar County CPS,* ___ So.3d ___, No. 2020-CA-70-COA,
2021 WL 4271909 (Miss. Ct. App. Sept. 21, 2021) 71

I. TERMINATION OF PARENTAL RIGHTS PROCEEDINGS 72
A. Physical abuse 72
1. *Coulter v. Dunn,* 312 So. 3d 713 (Miss. 2021) 72
B. Substance abuse 72
1. *M.A.S. v. Lamar County CPS,* ___ So.3d ___, 2021 WL
4271909 (Miss. Ct. App. No. 2020-CA-70-COA, decided 9/22/21) 72
C. Termination of Parental Rights Based on Abandonment 73
1. *Smith v. Doe,* 314 So. 3d 154 (Miss. Ct. App. 2021) 73

II. NEW PROCEDURES FOR REQUESTING YOUTH COURT
RECORDS FOR USE IN CHANCERY OR CIRCUIT COURT 73

A. PROCEDURES FOR OTHER COURTS TO OBTAIN YOUTH
COURT RECORDS 73
1. All Youth Court Records Concerning Children are Confidential 73
2. Forms from the First Chancery District 74

B. CHANCERY COURT PETITION FOR WRIT OF ASSISTANCE
TO OBTAIN YOUTH COURT RECORDS 74

C. PROPOSED SUBPOENA DUCES TECUM FOR YOUTH
COURT RECORDS 77

D. CHANCERY COURT ORDER GRANTING PETITION FOR
WRIT OF ASSISTANCE 79

E. YOUTH COURT MOTION FOR RELEASE OF YOUTH
COURT RECORDS TO CHANCERY COURT 80

F. YOUTH COURT ORDER AUTHORIZING LIMITED DISCLOSURE
OF YOUTH COURT RECORDS TO CHANCERY COURT SUBJECT
TO YOUTH COURT CONFIDENTIALITY RULES 84

III. APPEALS IN YOUTH COURT 86

    A. TIMELY APPEALS OF ALL ISSUES IN YOUTH COURT 86
        1. *E.K. V. Miss. Dept. of Child Protection Services*, 249 So.3d 377
        (Miss. 2018) 86
        2. *Interest of M.M.*, 319 So.3d 1188 (Miss. Ct. App. 2021) 87
        3. *Interest of K.M. v. Jackson County Youth Court*, ___ So.3d ___,
        2020 WL 7056087 (Miss. Ct. App. 2020) 87

    B. PREMATURE FILING OF THE NOTICE OF APPEAL FROM
    YOUTH COURT PROCEEDINGS 87
        1. *In the Interest of PXS, a Minor v. Adams County Youth Court*,
        ___ So.3d ___, 2022 WL 2037688 (Miss. Ct. App. decided 6/7/22) 87

    C. FAILURE TO TIMELY PERFECT APPEAL WITHIN 30 DAYS
    AFTER ENTRY OF THE YOUTH COURT ORDER 88
        1. *Interest of M.M.*, 319 So. 3d 1188 (Miss. Ct. App. 2021) 88

IV. YOUTH COURT PROCEDURES APPLY IN ABUSE/NEGLECT CASES IN
    CHANCERY COURT 89
    A. Rule 2(a), U.R.Y.C.P. 89
    B. Rule 8, U.R.Y.C.P. 90

V. MISCELLANEOUS LEGAL ISSUES 91
    A. IMMUNITY EXTENDED FOR GOOD FAITH REPORTS,
    INVESTIGATIONS AND JUDICIAL PROCEEDINGS CONCERNING
    CHILD ABUSE OR NEGLECT 91

    B. THE ADOPTION STATUTES WERE AMENDED BY 2022 MISS.
    LAWS S.B. 2263 TO SIMPLIFY ADULT ADOPTIONS 92

    C. THE PROHIBITION AGAINST ADOPTION BY SAME SEX COUPLES
    HAS BEEN DELETED FROM MISS. CODE ANN. § 93-17-3(5) 95

    D. DURABLE LEGAL CUSTODY 95
        1. *Interest of M.M.*, 319 So. 3d 1188 (Miss. Ct. App. 2021) 95
        2. *In the Interest of Kevin, a Minor, Shayla Taylor v. Miss. Dept.
        of Child Protection Services*, ___ So.3d ___, 2022 WL 2127320
        (Miss. Ct. App. decided 6/14/22) 96

    E. AUTHENTICATION AND ADMISSION OF SOCIAL MEDIA EVIDENCE 99
        1. *Webb v. State*, ___ So.3d ____, 2022 WL 1679114 (Miss.
        Case No. 2021-KA-00082- SCT, decided May 26, 2022) 99

David L. Calder, University of Miss. Child Advocacy Clinic
phone (662) 915-7394; e-mail: davidcalder23@gmail.com

I.   UPDATE ON GUARDIAN AD LITEM CASES.

A. ROLE OF THE GAL AS A LAY WITNESS.

1. *Summers v. Gros*, 319 So.3d 479 (Miss. 2021).
Unwed mother filed petition to modify temporary-custody order, and paternal grandparents, who had temporary custody, simultaneously filed motion to suspend visitation. The GAL recommended that there was insufficient evidence to rebut the presumption that the mother should have custody as the "natural parent." The chancellor rejected this recommendation based on the GAL's testimony that she "had not been aware of certain key facts relating to [mother's] lengthy failures to exercise meaningful visitation or provide monetary support for the child." The Chancellor concluded that child's best interest required that custody be awarded to his paternal grandparents, and mother appealed.
The Supreme Court affirmed, holding that:
(1) Although chancellor was aware of guardian ad litem's recommendations and the reasons for them, chancellor did not err when he reached a different conclusion, namely that grandparents were entitled to custody.
(2) **Although the chancellor's original order appointing a guardian ad litem designated that the GAL would testify as an "expert," the chancellor did not err when he subsequently removed that requirement, and held that the GAL would** *"testify as a guardian ad litem."*
(3) Mother failed to show manifest error or an abuse of discretion in the chancellor's finding that the natural-parent custody presumption had been overcome.

SIGNIFICANT ISSUES:
a. **EXPERT WITNESS DESIGNATION:** In *Summers*, the chancellor initially appointed the guardian ad litem to investigate as an "expert witness." However, as the case progressed, the chancellor **removed the expert designation**, and Ordered that the GAL would simply **"testify as a guardian ad litem."** The mother argued that this was improper. **However, the mother failed to properly brief this issue on appeal, so this issue was deemed waived by the MSSC.**

b. **GAL'S ROLE MAY CHANGE:** Although the issue was deemed waived, the MSSC addressed the merits of the mother's expert witness argument, and held that an Order appointing a GAL "should not permanently bind the court should needs change as the litigation progresses."

S.G. v. D.C., 13 So. 3d 269, 281 (Miss. 2009). The chancellor may expand or limit the role of a guardian ad litem "as the needs of a particular case dictate ...." Id. at 281. "The guardian ad litem may serve in a very limited purpose if the court finds such service necessary in the interest of justice[,]" and his or her "role at trial may vary depending on the needs of the particular case." Id. at 280-81.

c. GAL MAY OFFER OPINION TESTIMONY WITHOUT BEING DESIGNATED AS AN EXPERT. At trial, the mother tendered the guardian ad litem as an "expert witness," but the chancellor refused to recognize the GAL in that capacity, because **mother "was unable to explain what kind of an expert the guardian ad litem was supposed to be." The chancellor held that he would allow the guardian ad litem** *"to testify as a guardian ad litem."* The MSSC approved that decision. The Court explained that the mother failed to identify any proffered opinion testimony that was excluded by the trial court as a result of this ruling, or any other prejudice she suffered as a result of the chancellor's decision.

The principles set forth in *Summers v. Gros* establish that a GAL may offer opinion testimony by way of recommendations concerning the best interest of the child without being designated or qualified as an "expert witness." While this analysis is arguably *dicta*, since the Court held that the expert witness issue had been waived, because the mother failed to properly brief it on appeal, this could be relied on if there is an objection to a GAL offering opinion testimony because they are not qualified as an "expert." **This should be addressed in the Order of Guardian ad Litem Appointment that the Court issues.**

B. CASES RECOGNIZING THE GAL AS AN EXPERT WITNESS:

1. Rules 701-706, Miss.R.Evid.

Significantly, the holding in *Summers v. Gros* does not mention Rules 701-706, Miss.R.Evid., or the comment in footnote five of *S.G. v. D.C.*, or the prior decisions in *McDonald, Ballard,* or *Barber,* where the Court explicitly approved designation of the GAL as an "expert witness."

Rule 701 limits the opinion testimony of **"lay witnesses"** to that which is "(a) rationally based on the witness's perception; (b) helpful to clearly understanding the witness's testimony or to determining a fact in issue; and (c) not based on scientific, technical, or other specialized knowledge within the scope of Rule 702."

Rule 702 allows **opinion testimony by a person with "specialized knowledge or training."** The Comment to Rule 702 explains that through such opinion testimony, an expert witness may **"... take the next step of suggesting the inference which should be drawn from applying the specialized knowledge to the facts."** Making recommendations about the "best interest of a child" in a custody case is the type of opinion testimony that Rule 702 allows.

2. *S.G. v. D.C.*, 13 So.3d 269, 274 (Miss. 2009)

In *S.G. v. D.C.*, 13 So.3d 269, 274 (Miss. 2009) the MSSC noted that "the guardian ad litem issued a preliminary report **expressing numerous personal opinions**." In footnote five, the Court explained: "**The record reveals only one attempt to qualify the guardian ad litem to render such expert opinions.** The only qualification stated was that the guardian ad litem had served for many years as a guardian ad litem. In other words, the first time the guardian ad litem rendered such an opinion, he was not qualified, but thereafter, he was because he had done so before. **We find such meager qualifications unacceptable as a matter of law, under the principles set forth in Daubert v. Merrell Dow Pharms., 509 U.S. 579, 113 S.Ct. 2786, 125 L.Ed.2d 469 (1993) (adopted by this Court in Miss. Transp. Comm'n v. McLemore, 863 So.2d 31, 35–40 (Miss.2003)).**

3. *D.J.L. v. Bolivar County DHS ex rel. McDaniel*, 824 So.2d 617 (Miss.2002)

In *D.J.L. v. Bolivar County DHS ex rel. McDaniel*, 824 So.2d 617 (Miss.2002), the MSSC "emphatically proclaim[ed] to the bench and bar that ... the guardian must submit a written report to the court during the hearing, or testify and thereby become available for cross-examination by the natural parent." Id. at 623. **Therefore, the GAL would have been derelict in her duty to zealously represent the boys' best interests if she had failed to interview the boys, consider the opinions of experts, marshal evidence, make an independent recommendation, question witnesses, submit reports, and make herself available for cross-examination.**

4. *McDonald v. McDonald*, 39 So.3d 868, 883 (Miss. 2010)

In *McDonald v. McDonald*, 39 So.3d 868, 883 (Miss. 2010), the Majority opinion described the GAL's duties even though he had not been appointed as an expert witness. "The guardian ad litem shall investigate, make recommendations to the court or enter reports as necessary to hold paramount the child's best interest ...." The Court noted that this was "... consistent with the traditional roles required of a GAL, which predate the enactment of the statutes. Miss. Code Ann. § 43–21–121(3) (Rev.2009). In *In the Interest of D.K.L.*, 652 So.2d 184 (Miss.1995), this Court held that **a GAL had failed in his duties by simply deferring to a therapist's recommendations, and not submitting his own recommendation as to the best interests of a child.** Id. at 188. *See also M.J.S.H.S. v. Yalobusha County Dep't of Human Servs. ex rel. McDaniel*, 782 So.2d 737, 740–42 (Miss.2001) (GAL failed in his duty by relying on DHS records and the recommendations of a therapist and social worker, and by not making his own recommendations).

In the specially concurring majority opinion, in *McDonald*, a majority of the justices approved this statement: "Certainly I agree that **guardians ad litem—properly appointed under Rule 706 and qualified as experts under Rule 702—may rely on hearsay in reaching their opinions.** But hearsay used to support an expert's opinion is quite different from hearsay admitted as substantive evidence." *McDonald v. McDonald*, 39 So.3d 868, 887 (¶68) (Miss. 2010). The Court also held: "**Rule 1 of the Mississippi Rules of Evidence plainly says those**

rules apply in chancery court—and they include no exception for guardians ad litem." Id. "[G]uardians ad litem—properly appointed under Rule 706 and qualified as experts under Rule 703—may rely on hearsay in reaching their opinions. But hearsay used to support an expert's opinion is quite different from hearsay admitted as substantive evidence." Id. (¶68). In other words, "pure, rank, un-cross-examined hearsay" by a guardian ad litem cannot be used as substantive evidence. Id. (¶68).

5. *Ballard v. Ballard*, 255 So.3d 126, 133–34 (¶19) (Miss. 2017)

In *Ballard v. Ballard*, 255 So.3d 126, 133–34 (¶19) (Miss. 2017), the MSSC affirmed the holding in *McDonald* which set forth the "proper role" of a guardian ad litem to "... investigate the allegations before the court, process the information found, report all material information to the court, and (if requested) make a recommendation." The Court concluded: "The guardian ad litem plays an important role, and—as set forth above—chancellors must consider all of the information available to the guardian ad litem when considering whether to follow the recommendation made." The *Ballard* Court also noted that the specially concurring opinion approved by five justices carried "precedential value."

6. *Barber v. Barber*, 288 So.3d 325, 331-32 (¶27) (Miss. 2020)

In *Barber v. Barber*, 288 So.3d 325, 331-32 (¶27) (Miss. 2020), the MSSC recognized that when charges of child abuse or neglect arise, Miss. Code Ann. §93-5-23 and § 93-11-65(4) mandate the appointment of a guardian ad litem who is an attorney "to protect the interest[s] of the child[ren] for whom he has been appointed" and who is authorized to "investigate, make recommendations to the court or enter reports as necessary to hold paramount the child's best interest." The Court stated that under the standard established in *McDonald,* **"[w]hen a chancellor chooses to hear the abuse allegation during a custody hearing, appointment of a [guardian ad litem] is mandatory. As part of his or her duties, the [guardian ad litem] must either submit a written report or testify, and must make recommendations to the court if requested."** Id. at 332 (¶28).

In *Barber*, the Court "... emphasize[d] the serious and vital nature of guardians ad litem in safeguarding the welfare of children whose lives are impacted irrevocably by the decisions of our judicial system. ... [Miss. Code] Section 93-5-23 and this Court's decisions applying it make clear that **the legislature and the judiciary have recognized the specific need for an officer of the court with the dedicated role of protecting the interests of children who are the subject of child abuse or neglect allegations.** The appointment of a guardian ad litem is not a mere perfunctory hoop through which the court must go to resolve a child custody case. Rather, the role of the guardian ad litem is a meaningful one; it has been enshrined in the law and public policy of this state for the very reason that the guardian ad litem is the only participant in a child custody proceeding whose sole interest is identifying and protecting the rights of the children and reporting its findings to the court. Therefore, a chancellor's failure to consider a mandatorily appointed guardian ad litem's findings is an error of the utmost seriousness." Id. at 332 (¶29).

The MSSC held that "the chancellor's failure to address the guardian ad litem's report constitutes reversible error." Id. at 333 (¶31). The Court stated: "The guardian ad litem, the only officer of the court charged with the sole responsibility of guarding the legal interests of the children, was not called upon to provide her findings or recommendations to the trial court." Id. at 333 (¶36). "**When the court asked the guardian ad litem whether there was evidence of abuse, "[i]n your opinion, as the guardian ad litem[,]" she responded, "[y]es, your Honor."** Notwithstanding that unequivocal announcement, the chancellor granted the father's motion, and the children's guardian ad litem was excused from the trial." Id. at (¶36).

C. LIMITED ROLE FOR THE GAL
1. *Smith v. Smith*, 206 So.3d 502, 512 (¶23) (Miss. 2016)
The GAL can also clearly be appointed **only to serve in a limited investigatory role.** For example, in *Smith v. Smith*, 206 So.3d 502, 512 (¶23) (Miss. 2016), the Court approved the limited role the GAL was assigned, to investigate sexual abuse allegations, secure and coordinate appropriate expert witnesses, and make a recommendation on visitation, **but not on custody.** Similarly, in *Carter v. Carter*, 204 So.3d 803, 806 (¶12) (Miss. Ct. App. 2015), the GAL "... was appointed for a specific [limited] purpose—to investigate [the mother's] home environment — just as the supreme court contemplated in *S.G. v. D.C.*" (citing *S.G. v. D.C.*, 13 So.3d 269, 280–81 (¶47) (Miss. 2009).

PRACTICE NOTE: A guardian ad litem arguably has **"knowledge, skill, experience, training, and education"** as an attorney investigating cases, marshaling evidence, examining or cross-examining witnesses, researching and applying legal standards and principles, and adhering to the rules of evidence, the rules of civil procedure, and other court rules. Attorneys also regularly advocate for the "best interests" of our clients based on the facts discovered in the investigation. In addition, a GAL must receive the annual training approved by the Mississippi Judicial College for certification as a GAL under the statutory standards established in Miss. Code Ann. § 43-21-121(4). This training includes specific education about child protection and welfare. Arguably, all of this training, education, and experience this provides a basis for appointment as a "guardian ad litem expert witness" under Rules 702 and 706, Miss.R.Evid.

D. MANDATORY VS. DISCRETIONARY APPOINTMENT OF GAL.

1. *Gibson v. Gibson*, 333 So.3d 103 (Miss. Ct. App. 2022).
In a divorce action, the chancellor the chancellor appointed a guardian ad litem for the child, even though there were no allegations of abuse or neglect, so the GAL appointment was "discretionary" not "mandatory." After the GAL closed his law practice, the chancellor relieved him of any further responsibilities. The parents filed motions for appointment of a new GAL, but those requests were denied.

The chancellor awarded "guardianship" of the child to the father's sister and her husband (the Whiteheads), because the mother was incarcerated, and the child had been living with the Whiteheads for three years. Subsequently the trial court then entered an agreed judgment of divorce, but the parties did not address the issue of the guardianship or custody of the child. After the mother was released from jail, the trial court conducted a custody hearing and awarded **awarded paramount physical custody to the mother, with visitation rights to the father.** Father appealed.

The Court of Appeals affirmed, holding:

(1) GAL's appointment was **"discretionary" not "mandatory"** under the rules, and therefore, the GAL was not required for submit written report. The GAL did testify at a temporary hearing, and stated that **the father had been uncooperative in the investigation, and he did not feel obligated to try to "track him down" for an interview.**

(2) **The chancery court was not obligated to appoint another "discretionary" GAL after the initial GAL was relieved of his duties.**

(3) Because the appointment of the GAL in this case was "discretionary," the chancery court's decision to allow "the GAL to withdraw without submitting a final custody recommendation" did not constitute error.

2. *Warren v. Rhea*, 318 So. 3d 1187 (Miss. Ct. App. 2021).

Father filed for divorce, and both parties requested full custody of their child. During the proceedings, father alleged that the child had been abused by the mother, so a mandatory GAL was appointed. The court granted father a divorce after finding that he had proven the ground of habitual cruel and inhuman treatment, based on testimony about physical and domestic abuse. The chancellor ordered the parties to participate in parenting classes and reunification counseling. The child was also to receive counseling, but one facility refused to provide services because the wife was abusive and threatening toward the staff at the counseling center. At the trial, the child testified about the abuse he received from the mother.

The GAL concluded that the child had been physically and emotionally abused by the mother, who blamed the child for all of her marital troubles, and for the divorce. The GAL recommended that the father have custody, and that the mother be allowed visitation only after she participated in reunification counseling, and the counselor determined that it would be safe and in the child's best interest for him to spend time with his mother.

The Chancery Court granted the divorce, awarded father primary and legal custody of the child, but awarded reasonable unsupervised visitation rights to the mother, who also received an award of rehabilitative alimony in the amount of $750 a month for a period of 48 months. Husband appealed.

The Court of Appeals **reversed and remanded the chancellor's award of custody and visitation, because the chancellor failed to address and explain why the court deviated from mandatory guardian ad litem's findings and recommendations.** The chancery court's award of rehabilitative alimony was affirmed.

SIGNIFICANT ISSUES:

a. The guardian ad litem recommended that the father have custody of the couple's teenaged son, who had been physically and emotionally abused by his mother. The guardian stated that the boy was afraid of his mother and recommended that it was not in his best interest to visit with her. **She recommended that the mother not be awarded visitation unless the boy's counselor determined that it was safe and in his best interest to visit with her. The chancellor awarded custody to the father and "reasonable visitation" to the mother.** This was reversed because the chancellor deviated from the GAL's recommendations, **but failed to summarize the GAL's report, and state the reasons for deviating from the recommendations.**

3. *Savell v. Manning*, 325 So. 3d 1208 (Miss. Ct. App. 2021).

A chancellor did not err in refusing to appoint a guardian ad litem based on the mother's general allegation in a petition that the father **"failed to provide a safe environment"** and that their child returned from visitation **"in poor physical condition."** The Court held that the mother failed to provide specific facts to support her allegation of abuse or neglect, and therefore, a mandatory GAL appointment was not required.

4. *Embrey v. Young*, ___ So.3d. ___, 2021 WL 5576070 (Miss. Ct. App. No. 2021-CA-00091-COA, decided Nov. 30, 2021).

The court of appeals affirmed a chancellor's award of custody of a seven-year-old and two-year-old children to their mother. The court held that the chancellor was not required to appoint a mandatory guardian ad litem because the father did not request one, and the evidence presented at trial did not support a legitimate issue of abuse.

E. REBUTTING THE NATURAL PARENT PRESUMPTION FOR CUSTODY.

1. *Roberts v. Conner*, 332 So.3d 272 (Miss. Ct. App. 2021).

After death of the father who had physical custody of child under divorce decree, paternal grandmother and friends of father (the Conners) petitioned for emergency temporary custody and permanent custody of child, who was at that time in the custody of the mother, who lived in Florida. The Chancery Court granted *ex parte* a temporary restraining order (TRO) awarding emergency temporary custody to the father's friends, appointed a guardian ad litem (GAL), and after trial, awarded permanent custody to the Conners, and "in-state visitation" to mother. Mother appealed.

The Court of Appeals affirmed, holding:
(1) Grant of ex parte TRO awarding emergency temporary custody to father's friends was not abuse of discretion;
(2) Award of permanent custody to father's friends despite presumption favoring "natural" parent was not abuse of discretion, because the mother was deemed unfit;
(3) Substantial, credible evidence supported finding of mother's unfitness;
(4) Res judicata did not preclude consideration of child's educational records that predated the divorce decree;
(5) Award to mother of visitation rights only within the state was proper; and
(6) GAL fees paid by father's friends before trial were properly re-apportioned to mother.

SIGNIFICANT ISSUES:

1. The chancellor held that the petitioners rebutted the natural parent presumption by clear and convincing evidence, which justified placing permanent custody of the child with the father's friend, the Conners.

2. The chancellor properly concluded that the mother was "unfit" in four respects:
(1) **educational neglect** - - excessive absences and failing classes
(2) **medical neglect** - - cancelled tonsillectomy and failed to reschedule, and cancelled counseling sessions even though the child's father had recently died;
(3) failure to provide the child with **appropriate housing**; and
(4) mother's inability to provide for the **child's basic needs**, and failure to insure that the child maintained proper hygiene.

3. The mother was a resident of Florida, and the COA held that the chancellor properly restricted the mother's visitation rights to "in-state," meaning that she had to exercise her visitation in Mississippi. The COA rejected the mother's argument that specific findings of fact concerning danger to the child were required to justify such restriction on her visitation.

4. The COA approved the chancellor's visitation Order, stating: **"In this case, the judgment awarding custody stated in part that [mother] was "granted reasonable rights of visitation with the minor child, in the state of Mississippi, as may be agreed upon by the parties."**

5. The chancellor properly considered the child's educational records that predated the date of the divorce, as this was not barred by the usual application of the doctrine of *res judicata*.

6. The chancellor initially ordered the Conners to pre-pay $3,500.00 to cover the GAL's anticipated fees, and that any additional amounts would be submitted to the court for consideration. However, after the trial, the chancellor reapportioned the GAL fees by Ordering that the mother repay the Conners all that they had previously paid for the GAL's fees, and that the parties would equally split the remaining balance owed to the GAL. Thus the mother was required to reimburse the Conners for the money that they had already paid the GAL. **The COA noted tha the GAL's fees are considered "court costs," and this matter can be properly determined and assessed at the trial.**

2. *SUMMERS V. GROS*, 319 So.3d 479 (Miss. 2021)
The chancellor found that the natural-parent presumption had been overcome because, after the mother moved to Texas, she totally failed to exercise visitation with the child for extended periods of time. Haley also failed to support the child financially and failed to take an active role in the child's education and civic activities.

The natural-parent presumption may be rebutted by **clear and convincing evidence** that: '(1) the parent has abandoned the child; (2) the parent has deserted the child; (3) the parent's conduct is so immoral as to be detrimental to the child; or (4) the parent is unfit, mentally or otherwise, to have custody.'

"There is no bright-line rule defining *"desertion"* in the context of child custody. *See Patrick v. Boyd*, 198 So. 3d 436, 443 (Miss. Ct. App. 2016). Instead, desertion is "a factual question best left to the trial judge[.]" Davis, 126 So. 3d at 40."

THE TPR DEFINITION FOR "DESERTION" APPLIES TO CUSTODY.

In Summers v. Gros, the chancellor **cited the mother's failure to support the child, and her failure to exercise meaningful visitation over an extended period of time, as the underlying facts that supported his finding that the mother had deserted the child.**

The COA held that the definition of desertion as used in a custody case actually derives from the termination-of-parental rights cases. In *Davis v. Vaughn*, 126 So. 3d 33, 39 (Miss. 2013) the Court defined "desertion" as **"... foresaking one's duty as well as a breaking away from or breaking off associations with some matter involving a legal or moral obligation or some object of loyalty."** (internal quotation marks omitted). *Davis* was quoting *Petit v. Holifield*, 443 So. 2d 874, 878 (Miss. 1984), which was citing *Ainsworth v. Natural Father (In re Adoption of Minor Child)*, 414 So. 2d 417 (Miss. 1982), which were both adoption and termination-of-parental-rights cases.

The Court noted that the new statutory definition of desertion in the Mississippi Termination of Parental Rights Law (MTPRL), Miss. Code Ann. § 93-15-103(d) provides:
"Desertion" means:
(i) Any conduct by the parent over an extended period of time that **demonstrates a willful neglect or refusal to provide for the support and maintenance of the child; OR**
(ii) That the parent has not demonstrated, within a reasonable period of time after the birth of the child, a full commitment to the responsibilities of parenthood.

The Court recognized in Summers v Gros that the new definition of "desertion" in the MTPRL is in conflict with some earlier decisions where the Court had held that failure to pay child support, standing alone, does not constitute "desertion." See, e.g., In re Interest of J.D., 512 So. 2d 684, 686 (Miss. 1987) (" '[C]onstant arrearages in child support payments' do not constitute abandonment or desertion.") (quoting *Miller v. Arrington*, 412 So.2d 1175, 1178 (Miss. 1982))). But we are not required to decide that question today because this case involved much more than failure to pay child support.

Howwcver the MSSC affirmed the chancellor's finding that the mother 's lack of meaningful visitation and support over an extended period constituted desertion for the purpose of the custody statute. *Summers v. Gros*, 319 So.3d 479, 488–89 (Miss., 2021)

F. MODIFICATION OF CUSTODY - - MATERIAL CHANGE IN CIRCUMSTANCES STANDARD

1. *Kreppner v. Kreppner*, ___ So.3d ___, 2022 WL 841961 (Miss. Ct. App. Decided March 22, 2022)

Just a few months after agreeing to a divorce and custody order that severely limited her visitation with her daughter to every other weekend, the mother sought modification of the terms. The chancery court denied the motion, after finding that she had not met her burden of proving a material change in circumstances. Mother appealed.

The Court of Appeals affirmed, holding:

(1) The trial court acted within its discretion in declining to find a material change in circumstances based on father's marriage to his new wife, and

(2) The trial court acted within its discretion in denying mother's petition for modification of child custody on adverse-environment grounds.

SIGNIFICANT FACTS IN *KREPPNER*:

1. As part of the irreconcilable differences divorce decree, the mother agreed to a Custody Order that allowed her only supervised visitation with her child every other weekend. **Seven months after the divorce decree was entered, the mother filed for modification of custody, alleging that the father's new wife was interfering with mother's relationship with the child**. The parties then entered an Agreed Temporary Order that allowed the mother additional visitation without supervision, and required the parties to attend a co-parenting class. Mother then filed a second Petition for modification.

2. The chancellor **appointed a guardian ad litem, and a psychologist** to perform a forensic interview with the child and her family. Both recognized that the step-mother had a very hostile and adversarial relationship with the mother, and this caused the child to suffer anxiety and depression, because she had good relationships with both parents. **However, the COA held: "... it takes 'more than occasional unhappiness in a child' to warrant modification."**

3. The COA held that the mother failed to satisfy the traditional **"material change in circumstances"** test for modification, and that the alternative **"adverse environment"** test established in *Riley v. Doerner*, 677 So. 2d 740, 745 (Miss. 1996) did not apply to the facts presented in this case. Therefore, the mother's request for modification was denied.

2. *Carter v. Carter*, 324 So.3d 327 (Miss. Ct. App. 2021)

After their divorce, the parties shared **joint legal and physical custody** of their children, and the father was allowed visitation with the children every weekend. **Mother filed a motion to modify the child custody arrangement, alleging *father threatened mother and allowed children to roam the streets at night* when they were visiting father.** The Chancery Court found in favor of mother and reduced father's visitation from four weekends per month to two weekends. The chancellor also required each party to pay 50% of the guardian ad litem's fees. Father appealed proceeding pro se.

The COA held that the father's appeal was procedurally barred, because he failed to cite any case authority in his appellate brief. Although this case involved modification of an existing custody Order, there is no mention in the opinion of the traditional "material change in circumstances adverse to the best interest of the child test" that ordinarily applies in modification cases. The chancellor did conduct an *Albright* analysis, which is required under the second step of the "material change in circumstances test," and the mother prevailed under the *Albright* analysis.

The Court of Appeals affirmed the modification of custody, holding that:
(1) father's appeal was procedurally barred;
(2) questions father asked mother in interrogatories were irrelevant as to whether father put his children in danger, and thus questions were properly excluded;
(3) the chancery court's misstatement that father's stepson voluntarily left his mother's home did not constitute reversible error; and
(4) the father was required to pay one-half of the guardian ad litem's fees.

E.   IMPUTING OR ANTICIPATING CHILD ABUSE OR NEGLECT BASED ON THE FACTS AND CIRCUMSTANCES.

1. *Coulter v. Dunn*, 312 So. 3d 713 (Miss. 2021) (Imputed liability)
The supreme court affirmed a chancellors' termination of a mother's parental rights. Child Protective Services took custody of the nine-week-old child who was admitted to the hospital with a broken femur. **The treating physician, also a child abuse specialist, testified that in two months the child had suffered multiple severe injuries that could only have been caused by abuse,** including rib fractures, hip fracture, fractures above and below both knees, and ankle fractures.

The child lived with her paternal grandparents for four years, with the mother having supervised visitation. After four years, the grandparents sought to adopt her. **The chancellor found that the mother was responsible for her child's injuries, based on testimony that she was the only person with custody of the child during the time the various injuries occurred.**

The Court of Appeals affirmed, holding that **a trial court may infer that parents are responsible for abuse when they are the only persons with custody of a child. Responsibility for child abuse can be "imputed" to the parent who had custody of the child at the time the injuries were inflicted, even if there is no direct evidence.**

2. *Interest of K.M. v. Jackson County Youth Court,* ___ So.3d ___, 2020 WL 7056087 **(Miss. Ct. App. decided 12/01/2020) (anticipatory neglect)**

The parent's two older children were taken into custody by the DCPS on February 1, 2018 based on allegations of abuse and neglect. On July 31, 2018, DCPS was advised that the mother had given birth to K.M. On August 1, 2018, K.M. was placed in CPS's custody based upon the neglect of the mother's other two minor children under the theory of "anticipatory neglect." That same day a GAL was appointed for K.M.

On August 9, 2018, the Youth Court adjudicated the two older children as abused and neglected, and the court found aggravated circumstances that justified bypassing any reunification efforts. DCPS made clear at this time that they intended to seek termination of parental rights as to the two older children.

That same day the Youth Court also had a shelter hearing regarding the newborn child, K.M. Both the GAL and the prosecutor requested a bypass of reasonable efforts toward reunification. The Youth Court found that reasonable efforts toward reunification with the mother were not necessary due to the "history of this case."

On October 15, 2018, K.M. was adjudicated as an abused and neglected child based upon the theory of "anticipatory neglect." After a finding of aggravated abuse, the youth court found that reunification efforts were not necessary. Aggrieved, K.M.'s mother appealed.

SIGNIFICANT ISSUES:

a. **"Anticipatory Neglect" - - child neglect can be imputed to a parent based on the parent's past history of neglect with other children.**

b. The evidence was sufficient to support finding of aggravated circumstances as justification to bypass reasonable reunification efforts between the mother and the infant.

c. In Youth Court, a motion does not have to be filed to find aggravated circumstances as a justification to bypass reunification efforts between a parent and a child.

2. *In Interest of N.M. v. Mississippi Department of Human Services,* **215 So.3d 1007, 1013 (¶14) (Miss. Ct. App. 2017) (anticipatory or potential neglect)**

The COA stated that it could find no Mississippi case addressing whether a youth court may exercise jurisdiction over a newborn on the basis that the child''s siblings have been recently adjudicated as "neglected."

A few jurisdictions have determined that a court may have jurisdiction over a newborn under a theory of "anticipatory neglect," when another related child has been found to be neglected. Therefore, we believe that in a case involving evidence of neglect of a sibling, the Mississippi Supreme Court would adopt the doctrine of "anticipatory" or "potential" neglect, especially where the neglect of a sibling had been determined a mere month prior to the other child's birth.

Moreover, we find our Youth Court Act's definition of a "neglected child" is sufficiently comprehensive to include a newborn child whose parents have previously demonstrated that they are unwilling or unable to provide proper care for the child. The definition includes, inter alia, any child [w]ho is ... without proper care, custody, supervision or support" or "[w]ho, for any reason, lacks the care necessary for his health, morals or well-being." Miss. Code Ann. § 43–21–105(l)(ii) & (iv).

H. YOUTH COURT PROCEDURES AND NOTICE OF RIGHTS AT ADJUDICATION HEARINGS UNDER RULE 24, URYCP

1. *Interest of M.M.*, 319 So. 3d 1188 (Miss. Ct. App. 2021).

The court of appeals rejected a father's argument that a **youth court erred by failing to advise him of his rights, including the right to appeal**, as required by Miss. Code Ann. § 43-21-557(1)(e) ("At the beginning of each adjudicatory hearing, the youth court shall explain to the parties . . . the right to appeal). Even if the COA assumed that the Youth Court did fail to advse the parent of these rights, the Court held that this failure was, at best, merely harmless error, because the father was represented by counsel at the Adjudication Hearing and the Disposition Hearing. Father's attorney participated in the hearings and made no complaint about the failure to advise his client.

2. *M.A.S. v. Lamar County CPS*, No. 2020-CA-00070-COA, 2021 WL 4271909 (Miss. Ct. App. Sept. 21, 2021).

The court of appeals rejected a mother's argument that termination of her parental rights should be reversed because **the youth court failed to provide notice of her rights at the adjudicatory hearing,** failed to hold a separate disposition hearing, and did not advise her of her rights in the termination hearing until late in the proceedings. She also argued that the petition to adjudicate the children as neglected was insufficient to inform her of the basis for the petition. The court of appeals held that she waived arguments related to the adjudication and disposition hearings because she did not appeal from those orders. In addition, she waived arguments related to notice at the adjudication hearing and to the failure to hold a separate disposition hearing because she was represented by counsel at both hearings and made no objection. The court also held that failure to comply with the statutory notice requirements does not automatically require reversal. Because she was represented by counsel, the failure was harmless error at best.

The mother also argued that the youth court failed to advise her of her rights at the termination hearing at which she appeared pro se, waiting until several witnesses had been heard and evidence introduced. The court of appeals held that the youth court substantially complied with the requirements by providing notice during the proceedings and noted that the mother showed no prejudice as a result of the delay.

I. TERMINATION OF PARENTAL RIGHTS PROCEEDINGS

A. PHYSICAL ABUSE

1. *Coulter v. Dunn*, 312 So. 3d 713 (Miss. 2021).

The supreme court affirmed a chancellors' termination of a mother's parental rights. Child Protective Services took custody when the nine-week-old child was admitted to the hospital with a broken femur. The treating physician, also a child abuse specialist, testified that in two months the child had suffered multiple severe injuries that could only have been caused by abuse, including rib fractures, hip fracture, fractures above and below both knees, and ankle fractures.

The child lived with her paternal grandparents for four years, with the mother having supervised visitation. After four years, the grandparents sought to adopt her. **The chancellor found that the mother was responsible for her child's injuries, based on testimony that she was the only person with custody of the child during the time in which the injuries occurred.**

The court of appeals affirmed, holding that a court may infer that parents are responsible for abuse when they are the only persons with custody of a child, and they have no explanation for the child's injuries. Responsibility for abuse can be imputed to the parent who had custody of the child at the time the injuries were inflicted.

B. SUBSTANCE ABUSE

1. *M.A.S. v. Lamar County CPS*, ___ So.3d. ___, No. 2020-CA-00070-COA, 2021 WL 4271909 (Miss. Ct. App. Sept. 21, 2021).

Three children were removed from mother's home by DCPS based on reports of the mother's drug abuse and excessive school absences by the children. The Youth Court reunification plan required that mother take bi-monthly drug tests, and that she visit with the children, and become involved in their education. The children were returned to mother for ninety days on a trial home placement, but removed again when the mother tested positive for drugs. Over the next six months, mother refused to take any drug tests and did not exercise any visitation with the children. She did not attend family team meetings or respond to DCPS calls.

The Youth Court Ordered DCPS to discontinue reunification efforts and work toward adoption. Evidence at the termination hearing showed that two of the three children were born with drugs in their bodies, that the mother refused most drug tests, attempted to secure her own tests with a relative's urine, and tested positive when she were tested properly. She did not visit the children regularly, resulting in an erosion of the parent-child relationship.

The County Court Youth Court found that the mother's rights should be terminated based on habitual drug addiction that she was unable to control, and that contributed to a substantial erosion of the parent-child relationship. The Court of Appeals affirmed the termination of the mother's parental rights.

C. TERMINATION OF PARENTAL RIGHTS BASED ON ABANDONMENT.

1. *Smith v. Doe*, 314 So. 3d 154 (Miss. Ct. App. 2021).

The chancellor properly terminated the rights of a father who had not seen his seven-year-old son for five years, finding that the father had abandoned his son and that there was a substantial erosion of the parent-child relationship. The boy had been raised by his stepfather, who wanted to adopt him, and who the boy viewed as his father.

The court of appeals rejected the father's argument that he had not abandoned his son because he paid child support. The court also held that the boy's mother did not prevent him from seeing his son. He attempted unsuccessfully to work out a visitation plan with her outside of court. When the boy was one, she brought him to meet the father at a restaurant but refused to allow him to visit at his apartment. The father visited with the boy at a hotel nine months later when the child was almost two. Over the next five years, his only contact was to send Christmas presents in 2014. The gifts were returned. The father testified that he instructed his child support attorney to seek visitation, but the attorney delayed for two years. His attorney then withdrew, resulting in a delay of another year.

The guardian ad litem recommended termination based on the father's failure to visit with the boy in five years, resulting in a complete lack of a relationship between the two. The court of appeals affirmed the termination of parental rights. Abandonment may be proved by showing that on the date of the petition, the parent has deliberately made no contact with a child over the age of three for one year. The court did not accept the father's argument that the mother kept him from seeing his son or that, for five years, he relied on his attorneys to obtain visitation. He could have contacted the mother about visitation even though litigation was pending. In fact, she invited him to the boy's fifth birthday party, which he did not attend because of work. The court stated that "a mistaken belief that a parent was not allowed to contact another parent pending a termination of parental rights suit does not overcome a clear and convincing showing of abandonment."

II. NEW PROCEDURES FOR REQUESTING YOUTH COURT RECORDS FOR USE IN CHANCERY OR CIRCUIT COURT

A. PROCEDURES FOR OTHER COURTS TO OBTAIN YOUTH COURT RECORDS.

1. All Youth Court Records concerning children are confidential. The procedures that allow other courts to obtain these records are set forth in Rules 5 & 6 of the Uniform Rules of Youth Court Practice.

2. Forms from the First Chancery District.

The First Chancery District has posted a set of forms and instructions for the procedures to be followed in obtaining such records. These forms are available at: https://1stchanceryms.com/files-and-resources/ (last accessed on June 1, 2022).

B.   CHANCERY COURT PETITION FOR WRIT OF ASSISTANCE TO OBTAIN YOUTH COURT RECORDS.

IN THE CHANCERY COURT OF _____ COUNTY, MISSISSIPPI

_____

                                                                                          PLAINTIFF

v.   CAUSE NUMBER: _____

_____

                                                                                          DEFENDANT

PETITION FOR WRIT OF ASSISTANCE REQUESTING ISSUANCE OF SUBPOENAS DUCES TECUM CONCERNING YOUTH COURT RECORDS INVOLVING MINOR CHILD

Comes now, _____ the _____ of the minor child, _____, filing this Motion for Writ of Assistance, pursuant to Rule 6, U.R.Y.C.P., requesting the Court's assistance in the issuance of a Subpoenas Duces Tecum for Youth Court Records pertaining to the minor child named herein, stating as follows:

1. Plaintiff is the _____ of the minor child whose custody is at issue in the instant proceedings.

2. Previously, there was an investigation conducted by the by the _____ County Department of Child Protection Services [hereinafter: "DCPS"] concerning the minor child, _____.

3. There may have been a forensic interview conducted by a Child Advocacy Center, and proceedings in the Youth Court of _____ County concerning the minor child.

4. The minor child is now at the center of a contentious custody dispute in this Court.

5. The procedures for obtaining Youth Court Records for use in a Chancery Court proceeding are governed by Rule 6, U.R.Y.C.P. which provides:

(a) Procedures for issuing a subpoena duces tecum. No subpoena duces tecum for records involving children, as such records are defined under section 43-21-105 of the Mississippi Code, shall issue from any court other than youth court except upon compliance with the following procedures:

(1) the party shall make an application to the [chancery] court specifying which records are sought;

(2) the [chancery] court shall issue a subpoena duces tecum to the youth court for these records;

(3) the youth court, unless a hearing is conducted pursuant to Rule 6(b) of these rules, shall transfer copies of the records to the [chancery] court;

(4) the [chancery court shall conduct an in camera inspection of the records, in accordance with the procedures set forth in Pennsylvania v. Ritchie, 480 U.S. 39 (1987), to determine which records should be disclosed to the party;

(5) the [chancery] court shall, at all times, protect the confidentiality of the records to the extent required of the Youth Court under Mississippi's Youth Court Law.

(b) Hearing on access to confidential files. The youth court may require a hearing to determine whether the court or parties have a legitimate interest to be allowed access to the confidential files. In determining whether a person has a legitimate interest, the youth court shall consider the nature of the proceedings, the welfare and safety of the public, and the interest of the child.

Rule 6, U.R.Y.C.P. (emphasis added).

6. Under this rule, and the facts and circumstances presented in the case at bar, the undersigned respectfully requests that this Court issue a Subpoena Duces Tecum requesting that the Youth Court of _____ County order the production of all Youth Court Records concerning the minor child, _____, including any records filed with the Clerk of the Youth Court, any documents prepared by the Department of Child Protection Services, or a Child Advocacy Center, including any forensic interviews, to this Court for *in camera review*, so that this Court may determine whether this information should be released to the parties in the instant case.

7. Finally, the undersigned respectfully requests such other general relief as may be warranted in the premises.

8. The proposed Subpoenas Duces Tecum is attached to this motion as "Exhibit A."

Respectfully submitted, this the _____ day of _____, 20____.

Signature: _____

Address: _____

Phone: _____

E-mail: _____

CERTIFICATE OF SERVICE

I hereby certify that I have this day served via United States Mail, first class postage prepaid, and/or electronic service through e-mail, fax, and/or the MEC case filing system as provided under Rule 5 of the Mississippi Rules of Civil Procedure, a true and correct copy of the foregoing document to:

_____, Father or Attorney for Father
address

_____, Mother or Attorney for Mother
address

_____, Youth Court Prosecutor
address

_____, Youth Court Judge/Referee:
address

_____, Youth Court Clerk:
address

General Counsel for Miss. Dept. of Child Protection Services:
Kimberly G. Gore
General Counsel, MDCPS
750 North State St.
Jackson, MS 39202
P.O. Box 346
Jackson, MS 39205
Phone (601) 983-3095
E-mail: legaldocuments@mdcps.ms.gov
Kimberly.gore@mdcps.ms.gov

Respectfully submitted, this the _____ day of _____, 202___.

Signature: _____

C. PROPOSED SUBPOENA DUCES TECUM FOR YOUTH COURT RECORDS.

IN THE CHANCERY COURT OF _____ COUNTY, MISSISSIPPI

PETITIONER(S)

_____

vs.

CAUSE NO. _____

_____

RESPONDENT(S)

SUBPOENA DUCES TECUM IN SUPPORT OF
ORDER GRANTING WRIT OF ASSISTANCE

STATE OF MISSISSIPPI
COUNTY OF _____

TO: Youth Court of _____ County, Mississippi
        ATTN: Youth Court Judge/Referee _____
        address: _____

YOU ARE HEREBY requested, pursuant to the Order Granting Writ of Assistance that was issued by the Chancery Court of _____ County in Cause No. _____, and Rule 45(d)(2)(A), Miss.R.Civ.P., and Rule 6, U.R.Y.C.P., to produce within ten (10) days true and correct copies of any and all Youth Court records in your possession, or under your control concerning the following individuals:

1. All Documents identified herein pertaining to the following minor child/children:

NAME   DATE OF BIRTH

_____

_____

_____

_____

2. Youth Court Records under your control which are to be produced are as follows:
A. Youth Court records as defined in Miss. Code Ann. § 43-21-251 of Mississippi's Youth Court Law, including but not limited to any and all pleadings, orders, summonses, exhibits, physical evidence, witness lists, court and deposition transcripts, dockets, notices, papers, social records (including but not limited to social summaries, medical examination reports, and mental health examination reports) and Guardian ad Litem reports;
B. Forensic interviews conducted by a child advocacy center during any abuse or neglect investigation;

C. Law enforcement records as defined in Miss. Code Ann. § section 43-21-255 of Mississippi's Youth Court Law and including but not limited to any and all police reports, booking sheets, photographs, affidavits, grand jury indictments, audio and/or video records, physical evidence, medical records, oral and written statements, witness lists and forensic interviews;

D. Agency records as defined in Miss. Code Ann. § 43-21-257 of Mississippi's Youth Court Law and including but not limited to Department of Child Protection Services files;

E. Forensic Interviews as defined in Miss. Code Ann. § 43-21-105(u)(ii) (West 2021) of Mississippi's Youth Court Law, including but not limited to all video and audio recordings of forensic interviews prepared by an authorized Child Advocacy Center, and all related documents and materials; and

F. All other documents maintained by any representative of the state, county, municipality, or other public agency insofar as they relate to the custody, adjudication, or disposition of a child who is the subject of a youth court cause or a Mississippi Department of Child Protection Services investigation and which may be maintained in the records of the entity to whom this command is issued.

3. Unless a hearing is conducted by the Youth Court pursuant to Rule 5, U.R.Y.C.P., all Youth Court Records from the Youth Court Clerk, the Department of Child Protection Services, and any involved Child Advocacy Center shall be produced to the undersigned Chancellor for an *in camera* inspection in accordance with the procedures set forth in *Pennsylvania v. Ritchie*, 480 U.S. 39 (1987).

4. These records shall be delivered to Chancellor _____ (address) _____; phone: _____; fax: _____; e-mail: _____ within ten (10) days after receipt of this request pursuant to Rule 45(d)(2)(A), Miss.R.Civ.P. and Rule 6, U.R.Y.C.P.

5. Further, you are hereby requested to authorize the Mississippi Department of Child Protection Services, their Family Protection Specialist, Supervisor, Employees, Agents, or Forensic Interviewers assigned to these matters to appear and offer testimony regarding the Youth Court records relevant to the minor child(ren) at issue upon the matter being called for hearing before this Court.

HAVE YOU THEN AND HERE this writ, and fail not to comply under penalty of law. SO ISSUED, this the _____ day of _____, 20_____.

_____
CHANCELLOR

D. CHANCERY COURT ORDER GRANTING PETITION FOR WRIT OF ASSISTANCE.

IN THE CHANCERY COURT OF _____ COUNTY, MISSISSIPPI

_____

PLAINTIFF

VS.

CAUSE NO. _____

DEFENDANT

_____

ORDER GRANTING WRIT OF ASSISTANCE
FOR SUBPOENA DUCES TECUM
CONCERNING YOUTH COURT RECORDS

This cause comes before the Court on the Petition for Writ of Assistance which has been filed by _____ in this case. This Petition involves a request for Youth Court Records concerning the minor child _____, whose custody is at issue in this case. An investigation may have been conducted by the _____ County Department of Child Protection Serves (DCPS), concerning the minor child, and there may have been related proceedings in the Youth Court of _____ County, Mississippi.

Under Rule 6 of the Uniform Rules of Youth Court Practice, this Court may issue a subpoena duces tecum to the Youth Court of _____ County, requesting that all Youth Court Records be produced to this Court for in camera review, so that this Court can determine whether any information contained in those records should be disclosed to the parties in the instant case. The Youth Court Law makes clear that any disclosure of the Youth Court Records must be subject to the confidentiality rules established by the Youth Court Law. Under these circumstances, this Court is of the opinion that the request for Writ of Assistance is well-taken and should be granted.

Accordingly, it is hereby ORDERED that this Court will issue a subpoena duces tecum to the Youth Court of _____ County requesting that the Youth Court Records concerning the minor child, _____, be produced to this Court for *in camera* review. This Court will then determine whether any of these records will be disclosed to the parties in this case, subject to the rules of confidentiality that apply to these Records under the Youth Court Law.

So Ordered, Adjudged and Decreed, this the _____ day of _____, 20___.

_____
CHANCELLOR

E. YOUTH COURT MOTION FOR RELEASE OF YOUTH COURT RECORDS TO CHANCERY COURT.

IN THE YOUTH COURT OF _____ COUNTY, MISSISSIPPI

IN RE: _____, a minor
(date of birth _____)

Youth Court Case No. _____

MOTION FOR LIMITED RELEASE OF YOUTH COURT RECORDS
TO THE CHANCERY COURT OF _____ COUNTY

Comes now, _____, filing this Motion for Release of Youth Records concerning the minor child(ren) _____, stating as follows:

1. A custody action concerning the minor child(ren), _____, is pending in the Chancery Court of _____ County, Cause No. _____ before Chancellor _____.

2. A Motion for Writ of Assistance was filed in the Chancery Court pursuant to Rule 6, U.R.Y.C.P. requesting that the Chancery Court obtain copies of all Youth Court records concerning the minor child(ren), to determine if any of those Records are relevant to the Chancery Court proceedings.

3. The Chancery Court granted the Motion for Writ of Assistance and issued an Order dated _____ authorizing the issuance of a Subpoena Duces Tecum so that the Youth Court Records could be provided to the Chancellor for in camera review, as provided in Rule 6, U.R.Y.C.P. A copy of the Chancellor's Order is attached as "Exhibit A."

4. The Chancellor issued a Subpoena Duces Tecum in Support of the Order Granting Writ of Assistance requesting that all Youth Court Records concerning the minor child(ren) as defined by the Youth Court Law be provided to the Chancery Court, including Records from the Department of Child Protection Services, Records filed with the Youth Court Clerk, and Records prepared by a Child Advocacy Center, including forensic interviews, if any. A copy of the Subpoena Duces Tecum is attached as "Exhibit B."

5. Rule 6(a), U.R.Y.C.P. authorizes the disclosure of Youth Court Records to the judge of another Court in response to a Subpoena Duces Tecum issued by the Chancellor. Rule 5, U.R.Y.C.P. authorizes the Youth Court Judge to determine whether the disclosure of these Youth Court Records would be in the best interested of the minor child(ren).

6. Pursuant to Rule 6(a)(4), U.R.Y.C.P., these Youth Court Records are to be provided only to Chancellor _____ for in camera review, and a determination as to whether it would be in the best interest of the minor child(ren) for any of these Records to be disclosed to the parties in the Chancery Court proceedings.

7. The subject Youth Court Records are confidential under the Youth Court Law. Under Rule 6(a)(5), U.R.Y.C.P., any disclosure of these records to the parties in the Chancery Court

proceedings must be subject to the confidentiality provisions of the Youth Court Act. Miss. Code Ann. § 43-21-251 and § 43-21-261 (West 2021).

8. "Records concerning children" are defined under the Youth Court Act, Miss. Code Ann. § 43-21-105(u) (West 2021). These records include:

    a. Youth Court records as defined in Section 43-21-251

    b. Forensic interviews conducted by a child advocacy center

    c. Law enforcement records as defined in Section 43-21-255

    d. Agency records as defined in Section 43-21-257; and

    e. "all other documents" concerning a child who is the subject of a Youth Court proceeding.

Miss. Code Ann. § 43-21-105(u) (West 2021).

9. Miss. Code Ann. § 43-21-251(1) (West 2021) further defines youth court records as:

    a. The general docket of the Youth Court proceedings;

    b. All the papers and pleadings filed in the youth court cause;

    c. All social records of the Youth Court, including intake records, social summaries, medical examinations, mental health examinations, transfer studies and all other information obtained and prepared in the discharge of official duty for the youth court; and

    d. All documents, reports, and Orders filed in the Youth Court proceedings.

Miss. Code Ann. § 43-21-251(1) (West 2021).

10. All such "records concerning children" are designated "confidential" by the Youth Court Act, and disclosure is permitted only "as provided in Section 43-21-261." Miss. Code Ann. § 43-21-251(2) (West 2021).

11. Miss. Code Ann. § 43-21-261(1) specifically authorizes the disclosure of Youth Court Records to the judge of another court where a child custody action is pending, provided that the confidentiality of the records is preserved and protected in the other court. This statute provides in part:

(1) Except as otherwise provided in this section, records involving children shall not be disclosed, ... except pursuant to an order of the youth court specifying the person or persons to whom the records may be disclosed, the extent of the records which may be disclosed and the purpose of the disclosure. Such court orders for disclosure shall be limited to those instances in which the youth court concludes, in its discretion, that disclosure is required for the best interests of the child, the public safety, the functioning of the youth court, or to identify a person who knowingly made a false allegation of child abuse or neglect, and then only to the following persons:

... (b) The court of the parties in a child custody or adoption cause in another court; ....

Miss. Code Ann. § 43-21-261(1)(b) (West 2021) (emphasis added).

12. This includes the imposition of sanctions for civil contempt, Miss. Code Ann. § 43-21-153 (West 2021), and possible criminal liability in the event that the information in the Youth Court records is improperly disclosed. Miss. Code Ann. § 43-21-267 (West 2021).

13. Miss. Code Ann. § 43-21-267 (West 2021) provides:

(1) Any person who shall disclose or encourage the disclosure of any records involving children or the contents thereof without the proper authorization under this chapter shall be guilty of a misdemeanor and punished, upon conviction, by a fine of not more than one thousand dollars ($1,000.00) or by imprisonment in the county jail of not more than one (1) year or by both such fine and imprisonment.

(2) Nothing herein shall prevent the youth court from finding in civil contempt, as provided in Section 43-21-153, any person who shall disclose any records involving children or the contents thereof without the proper authorization under this chapter.

Miss. Code Ann. Miss. Code Ann. § 43-21-267 (West 2021) (emphasis added).

14. In addition, Miss. Code Ann. § 43-21-153 provides:

(1) The youth court shall have full power and authority to issue all writs and processes including injunctions necessary to the exercise of jurisdiction and to carrying out the purpose of this chapter.

(2) Any person who willfully violates, neglects or refuses to obey, perform or comply with any order of the youth court shall be in contempt of court and punished by a fine not to exceed five hundred dollars ($500.00) or by imprisonment in jail not to exceed ninety (90) days, or by both such fine and imprisonment.

Miss. Code Ann. § 43-21-153 (West 2021) (emphasis added).

15. The undersigned respectfully submits that the disclosure of the requested Youth Court Records is necessary, and in the best interest of the minor child(ren) in this case, so that the Chancery Court may be fully advised of all the facts, in order to take any appropriate action necessary to protect the safety and welfare of the child(ren) in the Chancery Court proceedings.

16. Under these circumstances, the undersigned respectfully submits that the requirements for release of the Youth Court records pertaining to the minor child(ren) to Chancellor _____ have been satisfied in this case.

17. Therefore, the undersigned respectfully requests that this Court issue an Order directing that these records be released in response to the Subpoenas Duces Tecum issued by Chancellor _____, who will review these records in camera and determine whether this information should be released to the parties in the Chancery Court proceedings. Any release of the Youth Court records by the Chancery Court will be subject to the requirement that the confidentiality of these records must be maintained at all times, as required under the Youth Court Law, by any persons who are granted access to these records in the Chancery Court proceedings.

18. The undersigned further requests such additional relief as may be warranted in the premises.

Respectfully submitted, this the _____ day of _____, 202____.

Signature: _____

Address: _____

Phone: _____

E-mail: _____

CERTIFICATE OF SERVICE

I hereby certify that I have this day served via United States Mail, first class postage prepaid, and/or electronic service through e-mail, fax, and/or the MEC case filing system as provided under Rule 5 of the Mississippi Rules of Civil Procedure, a true and correct copy of the foregoing document to:

_____, Father or Attorney for Father
address

_____, Mother or Attorney for Mother
address

_____, Youth Court Prosecutor
address

_____, County Youth Court Judge/Referee:
address

_____, Youth Court Clerk:
address

General Counsel for Miss. Dept. of Child Protection Services:
Kimberly G. Gore
General Counsel, MDCPS
750 North State St.
Jackson, MS 39202
P.O. Box 346
Jackson, MS 39205
Phone (601) 983-3095
E-mail: legaldocuments@mdcps.ms.gov
Kimberly.gore@mdcps.ms.gov

Respectfully submitted, this the _____ day of _____, 202___.

_____

xxxxxxxxxxxxx, MSB #_____

F. YOUTH COURT ORDER AUTHORIZING LIMITED DISCLOSURE OF YOUTH COURT RECORDS TO CHANCERY COURT, SUBJECT TO YOUTH COURT CONFIDENTIALITY RULES.

IN THE YOUTH COURT OF_____ COUNTY, MISSISSIPPI

IN RE: THE INTEREST OF:
_____, A MINOR
DATE OF BIRTH _____

CAUSE NO._____

**ORDER PERMITTING LIMITED DISCLOSURE
OF YOUTH COURT RECORDS TO THE
CHANCERY COURT OF _____ COUNTY**

ON THIS DAY, this cause came on to be heard upon the request for disclosure of certain records pertaining to the minor child named above, and this Court having heard and considered the same, does hereby find that this Court has authority under Miss. Code Ann. § 43-21-261(1) to order a limited disclosure of the child's records to Chancellor _____ of the Chancery Court of _____ County for use in proceedings in that Court concerning the minor child. The Court is of the opinion that this request for limited disclosure of Youth Court records is well-taken and should be sustained,

THEREFORE, IT IS HEREBY ORDERED that the Youth Court records involving the minor child named in the above styled cause shall be disclosed only as specified below:

1. The court, person, or agency to whom the records shall be disclosed is:

_____

_____.

2. The Youth Court records which shall be disclosed include:

A. Youth Court records as defined in Section 43-21-251 of Mississippi's Youth Court Law: Any and all pleadings, orders, summonses, exhibits, physical evidence, witness lists, court and deposition transcripts, dockets, notices and Guardian ad Litem reports;

B. Agency records as defined in Section 43-21-257 of Mississippi's Youth Court Law, including Department of Child Protection Services files, Guardian ad litem files, medical records and reports, psychiatric records and reports;

C. Law enforcement records as defined in Section 43-21-255 of Mississip pi's Youth Court Law: Any and all police reports, booking sheets, photographs, affidavits, grand jury indictments, audio and/or video records, physical evidence, medical records, oral and written statements, witness lists and forensic interviews; and

D. All other documents maintained by any representative of the state, county, municipality, or other public agency insofar as they relate to the custody, adjudication, or disposition of a child who is the subject of a youth court cause or a Mississippi Department of Child Protection Services investigation.

E. All other documents maintained by any representative of the state, county, municipality, or other public agency insofar as they relate to the custody, adjudication, or disposition of a child who is the subject of a youth court cause or a Mississippi Department of Child Protection Services investigation and which may be maintained in the records of the entity to whom this command is issued.

3. The purpose of the disclosure is: _____

_____

4. IT IS FURTHER ORDERED that pursuant to Miss. Code Ann. § 43-21-261(2), any records which are disclosed under this Order, and the contents thereof shall be kept confidential by the person or entity to whom the records are disclosed, except as provided in this order. Any further disclosure of any record involving the Child shall be made only under and by order of this Court or a Court receiving the records pursuant to the instant Order.

5. IT IS FURTHER ORDERED that the Family Protection Specialist(s), Supervisor(s), Employee(s), Agent(s), and Forensic Interviewers, employed by the Mississippi Department of Child Protection Services or any licensed Child Advocacy Center who have knowledge or prior involvement in matters pertaining to the minor child identified above shall be authorized to appear and offer testimony regarding the agency's records relevant to the minor child at issue upon the matter being called for hearing before the Chancery Court issuing a Subpoena Duces Tecum for the records being disclosed hereunder.

SO ORDERED, this the _____ day of _____, 20____.

_____
Youth Court Judge/Referee
_____ County

III.   APPEALS IN YOUTH COURT

A. TIMELY APPEAL OF ALL ISSUES IN YOUTH COURT

1. *E.K. V. Miss. Dept. of Child Protection Services*, 249 So.3d 377, 381 (¶13) (Miss. 2018)

In *E.K.* the MSSC initially noted that **"[t]his appeal arises from the Marion County Youth Court's adjudication of E.K. as a neglected child."** Id. at 378 (¶1). The adjudication and dispositions hearings were conducted on June 6, 2016. Id. at 380 (¶¶ 10-11).

On June 20, 2016, the Youth Court entered an emergency custody order, awarding custody of E.K. to the Marion County Department of Human Services pending a shelter hearing. Another emergency custody order awarded custody of E.K to DHS and ordered law enforcement officials to assist in locating E.K. At the shelter hearing held on June 28, 2016, the DCPS caseworker explained that E.K. could not be located initially, but on June 25, 2016, law enforcement officials found E.K. and DHS took custody of her. **At this same hearing, counsel for the parents questioned the sufficiency of the adjudication of E.K. as neglected.** Id. at 381 (¶12).

On July 1, 2016, The parents' attorney filed a Motion for interlocutory appeal to challenge the Youth Court's findings at the Adjudication Hearing. Id. at 381 (¶13). The Youth Court entered an Order allowing the interlocutory appeal of the June 6, 2016 Adjudication Order, but the MSSC denied the petition for interlocutory appeal. Id. at 381, n. 5 (¶13).

Subsequently, on February 17, 2017, the Youth Court again ordered the mother to submit to a hair-follicle test, which was completed on March 3, 2017. On April 3, 2017, the youth court entered a permanency order, returning custody of E.K to the parents. Id. at 381 (¶14).

The parents then appealed "... the sufficiency of the neglect petition, **the sufficiency of the evidence supporting adjudication, the lack of notice and service of process to [the parents] for the adjudication hearing,** several of the custody orders and the orders concerning the hair-follicle drug tests." Id. at 381 (¶15). **The MSSC held that "[t]he issues related to the adjudication order are dispositive of the appeal before us.** Id. at 381 (¶15).

The MSSC concluded: First, the mother did not knowingly or voluntarily waive her right to service of process or her right to representation of counsel for the Adjudication Hearing, and the subsequent Disposition Hearing by personally appearing at the hearing. In addition, there was no evidence that the father was notified about the Adjudication Hearing. Even though the mother was not properly before the court, and the father was not before the court at all, the Youth Court adjudicated their daughter neglected. Second, the neglect petition was legally insufficient to give notice to the parents of "the particular circumstances which w[ere to] be inquired into at the adjudicatory proceedings." Third, the evidence offered at the adjudicatory hearing of the child's status as neglected, was legally insufficient to support the neglect adjudication. Id. at 388-89 (¶48).

2. *Interest of M.M.*, 319 So.3d 1188, 1201 (¶40) (Miss. Ct. App. 2021)

The COA held: " 'The appellate standard of review for youth court proceedings is the same as that which we apply to appeals from chancery court. ...' " (citing *E.K. v. Miss. Dep't of Child Prot. Servs.*, 249 So. 3d 377, 381 (¶16) (Miss. 2018)).

3. *Interest of K.M. v. Jackson Cnty. Youth Court*, ___ So.3d. ___, 2020 WL 7056087 (¶9) (Miss. Ct. App. 2020).

"In youth court proceedings, the appellate standard of review is the same as we apply to appeals from chancery court. Questions concerning law are reviewed de novo." (citing *E. K. v. Miss. Dep't of Child Protection Servs.*, 249 So. 3d 377, 381 (¶16) (Miss. 2018). Id.

B. PREMATURE FILING OF THE NOTICE OF APPEAL.

1. *In the Interest of PXS, a Minor v. Adams County Youth Court*, ___ So.3d. ___, 2022 WL 2037688 (Miss. Ct. App. decided June 7, 2022).

In the Youth Court proceedings, the minor, PXS, was adjudicated to be a "child in need of supervision," based on the fact that he did not contest the allegations that were filed against him in the Petition filed by the Youth Court prosecutor. After the disposition hearing the minor filed *pro se* his "motion to set aside his *"guilty plea"* because he alleged that he had received ineffective assistance of counsel. The minor also filed his notice of appeal.

The COA stated: Rule 37 of the Uniform Rules of Youth Court Practice states that "[a]ppeals from final orders or decrees of the court shall be pursuant to the Mississippi Rules of Appellate Procedures." U.R.Y.C.P. 37. But the Mississippi Rules of Appellate Procedure do not specifically address the effect of undisposed-of post-trial motions in appeals from youth court. However, the rules do address undisposed-of post-trial motions in civil and criminal cases in Mississippi Rules of Appellate Procedure 4(d)-(e). **Whether a case is civil or criminal, a premature notice of appeal is deemed ineffective until the trial court rules on any pending post-judgment motion.** Phelps v. Phelps, 937 So. 2d 974, 977 (¶9) (Miss. Ct. App. 2006).

The COA noted that under the Uniform Rules of Youth Court Practice, there is no equivalent to a motion for a new trial in a civil case, see M.R.C.P. 59, or a motion for a new trial in a criminal case, see M.R.Cr.P. 25.1. The COA then concluded that in this case, the minor filed a post-disposition motion for modification, and then prematurely filed his notice of appeal. **Therefore, the youth court has had no opportunity to rule on the motion or consider any evidence that PXS may have presented or added in the record. Thus, the disposition order cannot be considered a "final order" ripe for appeal while the post-disposition motion is still pending in youth court. Accordingly, because it was premature, the COA dismissed PXS's appeal for lack of jurisdiction.**

C. FAILURE TO TIMELY PERFECT APPEAL WITHIN 30 DAYS AFTER ENTRY OF THE YOUTH COURT ORDER.

1. *Interest of M.M.***, 319 So. 3d 1188 (Miss. Ct. App. 2021)**

Three children were taken from their father's home based on a report that the house was filthy and uninhabitable, and that the children lacked access to adequate food and water to bathe. **On December 28, 2017, the children were adjudicated neglected, and a dispostion order was entered placing the children with their maternal grandfather.**

After a permanency review hearing on June 25, 2018, the court entered three separate permanency orders for M.M., C.M., and T.G.M. on **July 23, 2018.** The permanency orders placed the children in Durable Legal Custody with their grandfather. **On August 13, 2018, the father filed a single notice of appeal of the original adjudication order dated December 28, 2017, and the permanency orders and amended permanency order dated July 23, 2018.**

Shortly thereafter, the father was notified by the clerk's office that his appeal would require three separate notices, one for each minor child. On **October 31, 2018**, he filed a "motion to accept notice of an appeal filed out of time" as well as three separate notices of appeal pursuant to the clerk's instruction.

On May 15, 2019, the Youth Court entered an order allowing the appeal of the permanency orders and amended permanency order dated July 23, 2018, but not the original adjudication order dated December 28, 2017. On March 24, 2018, McCoy filed an additional notice of appeal of the youth court's order dated May 15, 2019, which denied his request for an out-of-time appeal of the Adjudication Order.

Father argued on appeal that he was entitled to have the time for appeal reopened for the Adjudication Order, because **he did not receive a copy of the Adjudication Order.** Therefore, he argued that he was entitled to have the time for appeal reopened pursuant to Rule 4(h) Mississippi Rule of Appellate Procedure 4(h). Further, he argued that **he was never told by his attorney or the youth court that he could appeal the adjudication order** as required by Mississippi Code Annotated section 43-21-557(1)(e)(v)(Rev. 2015). McCoy argues that the youth court's non-compliance with Mississippi Code Annotated section 43-21-557(1)(e)(v) constituted reversible error.

The COA held that the thirty day time limit for appealing the adjudication/disposition orders entered on December 28, 2017, was strictly enforced, and the father's notice of appeal and motions to re-open the time for appeal that were filed in August 2018 and 2019 were not eligible for relief under Rule 4(h), M.R.A.P., because more than 180 days had passed when he filed these motions. Specifically, in regard to the Adjudication Order, the COA held that the father did not file his notice of appeal until 229 days after the entry of the Order, and his Motion for out-of-time appeal was filed 307 days after the entry of the Adjudication Order.

The father also contended that the Youth Court failed to advise him of his right to appeal, as required by Mississippi Code Annotated section 43-21-557(1)(e)(v) which states: **"At the**

beginning of each adjudicatory hearing, the youth court shall ... explain to the parties ... the right to appeal." Since the father was represented by counsel at the Adjudication Hearing, the COA also rejected this claim, holding that "at best, this was harmless error."

SIGNIFICANT ISSUES:

    1. Durable legal custody may only be awarded to a person who has had physical custody of the children for six months under DCPS oversight.

    2. The Youth Court concluded that the father was unfit to have custody of the children, because **he failed to substantially complywith the Family Service Plan, specifically concerning the requirement that he enter a drug treatment program.**

    3. The court also rejected father's argument that the trial court should have engaged in an *Albright* analysis, which is not required when a court finds that a parent is unfit to have custody.

    4. The court also noted that he did not timely appeal the adjudication order in which the children were first placed with the maternal grandfather.

IV. YOUTH COURT PROCEDURES APPLY IN ABUSE/NEGLECT CASES IN CHANCERY COURT.

A. Rule 2(a), U.R.Y.C.P.

RULE 2 SCOPE OF RULES
(a) Proceedings subject to these rules. The following proceedings are subject to these rules:

        (1) any youth court proceeding;
        (2) any chancery court proceeding when hearing, pursuant to section 93-11-65 of the Mississippi Code, an allegation of abuse or neglect of a child that first arises in the course of a custody or maintenance action;
        (3) any proceeding conducted by a referee appointed pursuant to section 43-21-111 of the
        Mississippi Code;
        (4) any proceeding conducted by a designee appointed pursuant to the Mississippi Youth Court Law when acting in a judicial capacity.
(b) Commencement of proceedings. Proceedings commence when a report or complaint of a child within the jurisdiction of the youth court requires an action by the youth court **or by the chancery court** or by a referee appointed pursuant to section 43-21-111 of the Mississippi Code or by a designee appointed pursuant to the Mississippi Youth Court Law when acting in a judicial capacity.
(c) All orders of the court to be in substantial compliance with these rules. Courts conducting any proceedings subject to these rules shall utilize the Mississippi Youth Court Information Delivery System (MYCIDS) pursuant to sections 9-21-9 and 43-21-351 of the Mississippi Code.

COMMENTS AND PROCEDURES

Rule 2(a)(2).

Chancery court may hear an allegation of abuse or neglect of a child that first arises in the course of a custody or maintenance action when there has been no prior proceeding in youth court concerning that same child or, if there has been a prior proceeding in youth court concerning that same child, the youth court has terminated its jurisdiction of that case pursuant to the Mississippi Youth Court Law. See Miss. Code Ann. §§ 43-21-151(1)(c); 93-11-65(4) (2008); B.A.D. v. Finnegan, 82 So. 3d 608, 613 (Miss. 2012) ("Because the youth court had terminated its jurisdiction, there was no chance of conflicting orders and the like, as expressed in [K.M.K. v. S.L.M. ex rel. J.H., 775 So.2d 115 (Miss.2000)]."). All proceedings on the abuse and neglect charge shall be conducted in accordance with these rules.

B. Rule 8, U.R.Y.C.P.

(c) Chancery court proceedings. When a chancery court orders the Department of Human Services, Division of Family and Children's Services, or other appointed intake unit, to investigate a charge of abuse and neglect that first arises in the course of a custody or maintenance action, the assigned caseworker shall conduct an intake screening process in the same manner as required in child protection proceedings and thereupon recommend to the court:

(1) that the chancery court take no action;

(2) that an informal adjustment process be made;

(3) that the Department of Human Services, Division of Family and Children's Services, or other appointed intake unit, monitor the child, family and other children in the same environment;

(4) that the parents be warned or counseled informally; or

(5) that the matter be referred to the youth court prosecutor for consideration of initiating formal proceedings.

The chancery court shall then, without a hearing, order the appropriate action to be taken in accordance with Rule 9(b) of these rules. If the intake screening process discloses that a child needs emergency medical treatment, the judge may order the necessary treatment.

COMMENTS AND PROCEDURES

Rule 8(c) is to assure, consistent with Rule 2 of these rules, that chancery court procedures for investigating charges of abuse or neglect are consistent with those applicable to youth court. **When a chancellor orders the investigation of abuse or neglect, the Department of Human Services, Division of Family and Children's Services follows normal intake** procedures. **Upon receiving the intake recommendation, the chancery court must decide whether to hear the case or transfer it to youth court.** *If the chancery court decides to hear the case, then it must follow all procedures required of a youth court under these rules.*

V.   MISCELLANEOUS LEGAL ISSUES

A. IMMUNITY EXTENDED FOR GOOD FAITH REPORTS, INVESTIGATIONS AND JUDICIAL PROCEEDINGS CONCERNING CHILD ABUSE OR NEGLECT.

In 2021, the Mississippi legislature amended Miss. Code Ann. §43-21-355 to extend immunity for good faith reports of abuse or neglect to persons who participate in an investigation, evaluation, or judicial proceeding resulting from a report of abuse or neglect. It appears that this immunity would extend to Guardians ad Litem appointed by the Court. The legislation also extended immunity to Child Advocacy Centers and Multidisciplinary Teams acting in good faith and in the scope of their duties, so that they cannot be held liable for damages for making a referring a report of abuse or neglect, conducting an investigation, making an investigative judgment, or releasing or using information obtained in the investigation.

The amended portion of Miss. Code Ann. §43-21-355 (the general mandatory reporting statute) is highlighted below:

Any attorney, physician, dentist, intern, resident, nurse, psychologist, social worker, family protection worker, family protection specialist, child caregiver, minister, law enforcement officer, school attendance officer, public school district employee, nonpublic school employee, licensed professional counselor or any other person participating in the making of a required report pursuant to Section 43–21–353 or **participating in * * * an investigation, evaluation or judicial proceeding resulting * * * from the report shall be presumed to be acting in good faith**. Any person or institution reporting **or participating in an investigation, evaluation or judicial proceeding resulting from the report** in good faith shall be immune from any liability, civil or criminal, that might otherwise be incurred or imposed.

The amended portion of Miss. Code Ann. §43-15-51 provides:
... (6) A child advocacy center or a member of the multidisciplinary team is not liable for civil damages while acting within the scope of official team duties if the center or member, in good faith, refers a report of alleged child abuse for investigation, conducts an investigation, makes an investigative judgment or disposition, or releases or uses information for the purpose of protecting a child. The limitation of civil liability does not apply if a child advocacy center or multidisciplinary team member is not acting in good faith. The limitation of liability provided by this subsection for a child advocacy center or member of the multidisciplinary team, shall only

apply when the child advocacy center or the member is acting on behalf of or within the scope of duties for the multidisciplinary team as described in this section.

B. THE ADOPTION STATUTES WERE AMENDED BY 2022 MISS. LAWS S.B. 2263 TO SIMPLIFY ADULT ADOPTIONS.

1. Adults may be adopted under Mississippi law. Miss. Code. Ann. § 93-17-3(4) (West 2021) provides that "**Any person may be adopted** ... [and] [t]he word 'child' in this section shall be construed to refer to the person to be adopted, **though an adult.**" Adoption of an adult is a valid estate planning tool. *See In re Estate of Reid v. Pluskat*, 825 So.2d 1, 7 (¶22) (Miss. 2002).

2. Under the amendments enacted by 2022 Miss. Laws S.B. 2263, **as of July 1, 2022, in an Adult Adoption, the Chancellor may waive any Petition requirements under the Amended version of Miss. Code Ann. § 93-17-3(4), (5), (6) & (7) (effective July 1, 2022).**

3. Effective July 1, 2022, the prohibition against adoption by same sex couples will be deleted from Miss. Code Ann. § 93-17-3(5) (West 2021). *See Campaign for Southern Equality v. Mississippi Department of Human Services*, 175 F.Supp.3d 691, 694, (S.D. Miss. Mar. 31, 2016) (Case No. 3:15CV578-DPJ-FKB).

4. The amended version of Miss. Code Ann. § 93-17-3 provides:

(1) Except as otherwise provided in this section, a court of this state has jurisdiction over a proceeding for the adoption or readoption of a minor commenced under this chapter if:

(a) Immediately before commencement of the proceeding, the minor lived in this state with a parent, a guardian, a prospective adoptive parent or another person acting as parent, for at least six (6) consecutive months, excluding periods of temporary absence, or, in the case of a minor under six (6) months of age, lived in this state from soon after birth with any of those individuals and there is available in this state substantial evidence concerning the minor's present or future care;

(b) Immediately before commencement of the proceeding, the prospective adoptive parent lived in this state for at least six (6) consecutive months, excluding periods of temporary absence, and there is available in this state substantial evidence concerning the minor's present or future care;

(c) The agency that placed the minor for adoption is licensed in this state and it is in the best interest of the minor that a court of this state assume jurisdiction because:

(i) The minor and the minor's parents, or the minor and the prospective adoptive parent, have a significant connection with this state; and

(ii) There is available in this state substantial evidence concerning the minor's present or future care;

(d) The minor and the prospective adoptive parent or parents are physically present in this state and the minor has been abandoned or it is necessary in an emergency to protect the minor because the minor has been subjected to or threatened with mistreatment or abuse or is otherwise neglected, and the prospective adoptive parent or parents, if not residing in Mississippi, have completed and provided the court with a satisfactory Interstate Compact for Placement of Children (ICPC) home study and accompanying forms;

(e) It appears that no other state would have jurisdiction under prerequisites substantially in accordance with paragraphs (a) through (d), or another state has declined to exercise jurisdiction on the ground that this state is the more appropriate forum to hear a petition for adoption of the minor, and it is in the best interest of the minor that a court of this state assume jurisdiction; or

(f) The child has been adopted in a foreign country, the agency that placed the minor for adoption is licensed in this state, and it is in the best interest of the child to be readopted in a court of this state having jurisdiction.

(2) A court of this state may not exercise jurisdiction over a proceeding for adoption of a minor if, at the time the petition for adoption is filed, a proceeding concerning the custody or adoption of the minor is pending in a court of another state exercising jurisdiction substantially in conformity with the Uniform Child Custody Jurisdiction Act or this section unless the proceeding is stayed by the court of the other state.

(3) If a court of another state has issued a decree or order concerning the custody of a minor who may be the subject of a proceeding for adoption in this state, a court of this state may not exercise jurisdiction over a proceeding for adoption of the minor unless:

(a) The court of this state finds that the court of the state which issued the decree or order:

(i) Does not have continuing jurisdiction to modify the decree or order under jurisdictional prerequisites substantially in accordance with the Uniform Child Custody Jurisdiction Act or has declined to assume jurisdiction to modify the decree or order; or

(ii) Does not have jurisdiction over a proceeding for adoption substantially in conformity with subsection (1)(a) through (d) or has declined to assume jurisdiction over a proceeding for adoption; and

(b) The court of this state has jurisdiction over the proceeding.

(4) Any person may be adopted in accordance with the provisions of this chapter in term time or in vacation by an unmarried adult, by a married person whose spouse joins in the petition, by a married person whose spouse does not join in the petition because such spouse does not cohabit or reside with the petitioning spouse, and in any circumstances determined by the court that the adoption is in the best interest of the child. Only the consenting adult will be a legal parent of the child. The adoption shall be by sworn petition filed in the chancery court of the county in which the adopting petitioner or petitioners reside or in which the child to be adopted resides or was born, or was found when it was abandoned or deserted, or in which the home is located to which the child has been surrendered by a person authorized to so do. The petition shall be accompanied by a doctor's or nurse practitioner's certificate showing the physical and mental condition of the child to be adopted and a sworn statement of all property, if any, owned by the child. In addition, the petition shall be accompanied by affidavits of the petitioner or petitioners stating the amount of the service fees charged by any adoption agencies or adoption facilitators used by the petitioner or petitioners and any other expenses paid by the

petitioner or petitioners in the adoption process as of the time of filing the petition. If the doctor's or nurse practitioner's certificate indicates any abnormal mental or physical condition or defect, the condition or defect shall not, in the discretion of the chancellor, bar the adoption of the child if the adopting parent or parents file an affidavit stating full and complete knowledge of the condition or defect and stating a desire to adopt the child, notwithstanding the condition or defect. The court shall have the power to change the name of the child as a part of the adoption proceedings. The word "child" in this section shall be construed to refer to the person to be adopted, though an adult.

(5) No person may be placed in the home of or adopted by the prospective adopting parties before a court-ordered or voluntary home study is satisfactorily completed by a licensed adoption agency, a licensed, experienced social worker approved by the chancery court, a court-appointed guardian ad litem that has knowledge or training in conducting home studies if so directed by the court, or by the Department of Human Services on the prospective adoptive parties if required by Section 93–17–11.

(6) No person may be adopted by a person or persons who reside outside the State of Mississippi unless the provisions of the Interstate Compact for Placement of Children (Section 43–18–1 et seq.) have been complied with. In such cases Forms 100A, 100B (if applicable) and evidence of Interstate Compact for Placement of Children approval shall be added to the permanent adoption record file within one (1) month of the placement, and a minimum of two (2) post-placement reports conducted by a licensed child-placing agency shall be provided to the Mississippi Department of Child Protection Services Interstate Compact for Placement of Children office.

(7) No person may be adopted unless the provisions of the Indian Child Welfare Act (ICWA) have been complied with, if applicable. When applicable, proof of compliance shall be included in the court adoption file prior to finalization of the adoption. If not applicable, a written statement or paragraph in the petition for adoption shall be included in the adoption petition stating that the provisions of ICWA do not apply before finalization.

(8) The readoption of a child who has automatically acquired United States citizenship following an adoption in a foreign country and who possesses a Certificate of Citizenship in accordance with the Child Citizenship Act, CAA, Public Law 106–395, may be given full force and effect in a readoption proceeding conducted by a court of competent jurisdiction in this state by compliance with the Mississippi Registration of Foreign Adoptions Act, Article 9 of this chapter.

(9) For adult adoptees who consent to the adoption, a chancellor may waive any of the petition requirements and procedural requirements within subsections (4), (5), (6) and (7) of this section.

SECTION 2. [NEW - Classification pending]
For purposes of this act, the following words shall have the meanings ascribed herein unless the context otherwise requires:

(a) "Change of name petition" means a petition to change the legal name of an individual.

(b) "Offender" means any physically incarcerated person convicted of a crime or offense under the laws and ordinances of the state and its political subdivisions or the laws and regulations of the federal government.

SECTION 3. [NEW - Classification pending]
(1)   **(a) No offender shall have standing to file a change of name petition with the chancery court;**
(b) No chancellor shall grant a change of name petition for an offender; and
(c) No chancery clerk shall file a change of name petition for an offender.
(2) A chancellor may change the name of an offender if:
(a) A district attorney files a change of name petition on behalf of an offender;
(b) A sheriff of a county in which a person is incarcerated files a change of name petition on behalf of an offender;
(c) The Commissioner of the Mississippi Department of Corrections, or his or her designee, files a change of name petition on behalf of an offender; or
(d) A Mississippi Department of Corrections Chaplain files a change of name petition on behalf of an offender.

SECTION 4. This act shall take effect and be in force from and after July 1, 2022.

C. THE PROHIBITION AGAINST ADOPTION BY SAME SEX COUPLES HAS BEEN DELETED FROM MISS. CODE ANN. § 93-17-3(5) (WEST 2021).

D. DURABLE LEGAL CUSTODY

1. *Interest of M.M.*, 319 So. 3d 1188 (Miss. Ct. App. 2021)
The children were taken from their father's home based on a report that the house was filthy and uninhabitable and that the children lacked access to adequate food and water to bathe. The children were adjudicated neglected and placed with their maternal grandfather.

The father agreed to correct deficiencies in the home, submit to drug testing, enroll in counseling, and participate in the family drug court program. The drug court staff, the youth court judge, and DCPS recommended that he enter a treatment program for overuse of fentynal and that he pursue surgical options for pain relief. The father insisted that he did not need treatment for drug addiction, and he failed to substantially comply with the Family Service Plan that DCPS had prepared.

After six months, DCPS and the GAL recommended changing the family service plan to permanent placement in "durable legal custody," and the children were placed with their maternal grandfather. The COA rejected the father's argument that DCPS did not make clear to him that a failure to enter a drug treatment program would result in a loss of his children. The Court also rejected his argument that the Court should have considered placing the children with one of his relatives.

SIGNIFICANT ISSUES:

(1) Durable legal custody may only be awarded to a person who has had physical custody of the children for six months under DCPS oversight.

(2) The Youth Court concluded that the father was unfit to have custody of the children, because he failed to substantially comply with the Family Service Plan requirement that he enter a drug treatment program. **The Youth Court found that the father was unfit and unable to care for his children as a result of his addiction to opiates.**

(3) The Court rejected father's argument that the trial court should have engaged in an *Albright* analysis, which is not required when a court finds that a parent is unfit to have custody.

(4) The Court also rejected father's claim that DCPS had failed to explain the requirements of his DCPS Family Service Plan, and failed to exercise *"reasonable efforts"* to assist him in completing his Family Service Plan.

(5) The court also noted that he did not timely appeal the adjudication order in which the children were first placed with the maternal grandfather.

2. *In the Interest of Kevin, a Minor, Shayla Taylor v. Miss. Dept. Of Child Protection Services*, ___ So.3d ___, 2022 WL 2127320 (Miss. Ct. App. decided June 14, 2022).

Taylor (mother) appealed the Youth Court's decision to award durable legal custody of her son, Kevin, to his paternal grandparents. Specifically, she claimed that the Youth Court failed to comply with certain statutory requirements for an adjudication hearing, and that the Youth Court erroneously bypassed required efforts to reunify the child with her.

The facts in this case revealed that the mother had sent a video to Clark, the father of Kevin's half-brother, John, showing her brushing a knife against John's leg, and threatening to kill herself and John. There was no evidence that Kevin was present when Taylor "brushed" the knife against John's leg. At the time of this incident, Kevin was four years old and John was two months old. The mother was hospitalized for mental treatment after that incident.

At John's shelter hearing, DCPS learned of Taylor's other child Kevin, who was still in the home. DCPS took Kevin into custody and the Youth Court held a separate shelter hearing for Kevin, who was placed with his paternal grandparents. In removing custody, the Youth Court reasoned that keeping Kevin in Taylor's home "would be contrary to [his] welfare" because "the home environment or the people [in his home] pose an immediate danger." The Youth Court held that Kevin was removed from the home because he was "endangered" or "would be endangered" if he remained there.

The Youth Court Petition alleged that Kevin was an "emotionally abused child for purposes of section 43-21-105(m) of Mississippi's Youth Court Law." A combined adjudication hearing was held for both Kevin and John, and neither parent contested the allegations in the Petitions, so the children were adjudicated as "abused within the meaning of the Youth Court Act. Kevin's placement continued with his paternal grandparents.

After Taylor received psychiatric care, her condition improved, and DCPS recommended a Plan of Reunification for Taylor and Kevin. However, the GAL expressed her concerns about returning custody of the child to Taylor. The Youth Court judge agreed, and stated that **"the law**

... requires this Court to bypass reasonable efforts to reunite a parent that has subjected a child to abuse or torture." Ultimately, the Court elected to bypass reunification efforts between Taylor and both of her children. **The court also ordered a permanent plan of durable legal custody for Kevin.**

SERVICE OF PROCESS.

The Court noted that there was there was no indication in the record that the youth court ascertained whether notice requirements for the mother had been complied with, as required by section 43-21-557(c). However, the mother and her attorney were present at the hearing, and the attorney made no objection concerning service of process. Miss. Code Ann. § 43-21-507(2) (Rev. 2015) provides that **"[a] party other than the child may waive service of summons on [her]self ... by voluntary appearance at the hearing ...."** Thus, "[a]ny infirmity in the service was cured by [Taylor's] appearance at the hearing." *See In re J.P.*, 151 So. 3d 204, 210 (¶17) (Miss. 2014) (holding that father's appearance at hearing cured any potential defect regarding section 43-21-557(c)'s notice requirements). (¶11).

PRACTICE NOTES:

a. This holding appears inconsistent with the MSSC holding in *E.K. v. Mississippi Department of Child Protection Services*, 249 So.3d 377, 384 (¶27) (Miss. 2018), where the Court stated: "It is clear that [the mother] was present at the adjudicatory hearing and the initial disposition hearing. **Still, her presence alone is not enough to find that she waived her right to service of process.** *Even a cursory review of the record reveals that the youth court did not engage [the mother] on the record to determine if she waived her rights under either Section 43-21-507 or Section 43-21-557.*"

b. **BYPASSING "REASONABLE EFFORTS" TO REUNIFY THE FAMILY.**
The Court of Appeals affirmed stating that **DCPS properly bypassed the usual requirement that DCPS exercise "reasonable efforts" to reunify the child with the mother, as provided in Miss. Code Ann. § 43-21-603(7)(c)(iv) (West 2016):**

> (7) If the youth court orders that the custody or supervision of a child who has been adjudicated abused or neglected be placed with the Department of Human Services or any other person or public or private agency, other than the child's parent, guardian or custodian, the youth court shall find and the disposition order shall recite that:
>
> ...
>
> > (c) **Reasonable efforts to maintain the child within his home shall not be required if the court determines that:**
> >
> > ....
> >
> > > (iv) **That the effect of the continuation of the child's residence within his own home would be contrary to the welfare of the child and that placement of the child in foster care is in the best interests of the child.**

In the Interest of Kevin, 2022 WL 2127320 (¶14).

SIGNIFICANT ISSUES:

a. In the reported decision, the COA omitted critical parts of this section of the Disposition Statute, **Miss. Code Ann. §43-21-603(7)(c),** that allows DCPS to **"bypass reasonable efforts"** to reunify the child with the parents. This relevant portion of this statute provides:

> (c) **Reasonable efforts** to maintain the child within his home *shall not be required* **if the court determines that**:
>> (i) **The parent has subjected the child to aggravated circumstances**, including, but not limited to, **abandonment, torture, chronic abuse and sexual abuse**; *OR*
>> (ii) The parent has been convicted of **murder of another child** of that parent, voluntary manslaughter of another child of that parent, aided or abetted, attempted, conspired or solicited to commit that murder or voluntary manslaughter, or **a felony assault that results in the serious bodily injury to the surviving child or another child of that parent**; *OR*
>> (iii) The parental rights of the parent to a sibling have been terminated involuntarily; *AND*
>> (iv) That the effect of the continuation of the child's residence within his own home would be contrary to the welfare of the child and that placement of the child in foster care is in the best interests of the child.

Miss. Code Ann. § 43-21-603(c) (West 2021) (emphasis added).

The felony child abuse statute (which is referenced in the clearly requires that in order to bypass reasonable efforts to reunify a child with his family, the Youth Court must make factual findings under one of the subsections (i), (ii), or (iii) *AND* a factual finding under subsection (iv) that the continuation of the child within his own home would not be in his best interests. Finding only subsection (iv) does not appear to comply with the statute,

b. **Service of Process**

The COA acknowledged that "there is no indication in the record that the youth court ascertained whether notice requirements for Taylor had been complied with, as required by section 43-21-557(c)." However, since both Taylor and her attorney were present at the hearing, and Taylor's attorney made no objection concerning service of process, the COA held that this was not an issue, because Miss. Code Ann. § 43-21-507(2) provides that "[a] party other than the child may waive service of summons in writing, or ... by voluntary appearance at the hearing ...." Thus, the COA concluded that "[a]ny infirmity in the service was cured by [Taylor's] appearance at the hearing." *See In re J.P.*, 151 So. 3d 204, 210 (¶17) (Miss. 2014) (holding that father's appearance at hearing cured any potential defect regarding section 43-21-557(c)'s notice requirements).

This holding appears to be inconsistent with the holding in *E.K. v. Mississippi Department of Child Protection Services*, 249 So.3d 377, 384 (¶27) (Miss. 2018), where the **MSSC has held that waiver of service of process for an Adjudicatory Hearing must be in writing, or if the party appears, the issue of waiver must be clearly stated on the record.**

The MSSC stated: "It is clear that [the mother], though, was present at the adjudicatory hearing and the initial disposition hearing. **Still, her presence alone is not enough to find that she waived her right to service of process. Even a cursory review of the record reveals that the youth court did not engage Elizabeth on the record to determine if she waived her rights under either Section 43-21-507 or Section 43-21-557.**" Id. at 384 (¶27).

Other cases:
1. *Interest of M.M.*, 220 So.3d 285, 288 (Miss. Ct. App. 2017) ("Even if the mother had actual notice of the hearing via her conversations with the MDHS employee, actual notice is insufficient to cure a jurisdictional defect in service of process.")

2. *J.P.*, 151 So.3d 204, 210 (¶17) (Miss. 2014) ("The youth court is without jurisdiction unless the parents or guardian if available, be summoned as required by statute.") (Reversed on grounds other than lack of notice to the parent)

3. *In re N.W.*, 978 So.2d 649, 654 (Miss. 2008) (The Court reversed the adjudication by the Youth Court under Miss. Code Ann. § 43-21-557, because the father lacked notice of the hearing, even though the mother was present at the adjudication hearing.

E. AUTHENTICATION AND ADMISSION OF SOCIAL MEDIA EVIDENCE.

1. *Webb v. State*, ___ So.3d ____, 2022 WL 1679114 (Miss. Case No. 2021-KA-00082-SCT, decided May 26, 2022).

This case involved the criminal prosecution for of Webb for fondling and three counts of sexual battery of two underage girls. Webb was convicted of four felony counts, and these convictions were affirmed by the MSSC. At his trial, social media evidence was introduced which showed his communications with the girls.

The MSSC held that:
(1) The trial judge functions as the *"initial gatekeeper"* who determines the reliability of the social media evidence by requiring a *prima facie* case for authentication.

(2) A *prima facie* case authenticating social media evidence must be established through testimony from a witness with knowledge that "an item is what it is claimed to be." MRE 901(b)(1).

(3) "The fact that an electronic communication on its face purports to originate from a certain person's social networking account is generally insufficient standing alone to authenticate that person as the author of the communications." *Smith v. State*, 136 So. 3d 424, 433 (Miss. 2014).

(4) "Something more is needed" to show authorship. such as:
  • the purported sender admits authorship
  • the purported sender is seen composing the communication
  • business records of an internet service provider or cell phone company show that the communication originated from the purported sender's personal computer or cell phone under circumstances in which it is reasonable to believe that only the purported sender would have access to the computer or cell phone
  • the communication contains information that only the purported sender could be expected to know
  • the purported sender responds to an exchange in such a way as to indicate circumstantially that he was in fact the author of the communication
  • **other circumstances peculiar to the particular case may suffice to establish a prima facie showing of authenticity**

(5) Once a prima facie showing of authenticity is made, the jury the assesses the weight and credibility of the admitted evidence, including a factual determination of whether the purported user actually sent the message.

a. Admission of Screenshots of Snapchat Communications

1. Snapchat is a popular messaging app that lets users exchange photographs, videos, and text messages (called snaps). The primary distinction between Snapchat and typical text messaging is that the images and messages contained in a Snapchat (snaps) disappear after being viewed by the recipient. Although Snapchat automatically deletes photos and messages, a recipient of the snap can save one-on-one chats by taking a screenshot of the message or photograph. This can be accomplished using a smartphone's screenshot function or by using a separate device to photograph the message.

2. The victim's mother accessed her daughter's Snapchat account on her phone, and took screenshots of photos and messages exchanged between the Defendant and the child before the images disappeared. **At trial, the defendant sought to exclude the screenshot messages that were introduced against him, which included a photo of him with the child, their plans to marry, and a text message from the child asking the defendant to "shoot her mother."**

3. The defendant argued that the screenshots were not properly authenticated because (1) they were taken by the child's mother, who was a non-testifying witness, and (2) someone else could have accessed his phone to send the messages.

b.   AUTHENTICATING SOCIAL MEDIA EVIDENCE

1. The standards for authenticating electronic social media information were set forth in *Smith v. State*, 136 So. 3d 424, 432 (Miss. 2014).

2. Under MRE 901, the proponent must offer a foundation from which the jury could reasonably find the evidence is what the proponent says it is.

3. A proper foundation to establish a prima facie showing of the authenticity of social media evidence under MRE 901 can be accomplished by someone with knowledge that the item is what it is claimed to be.

4. Because of concerns about fabricating social networking applications and other similar evidence, "something more" than just a photo and account name is required to make a **prima facie case of authentication**. *Webb v. State*, ___ So.3d ____, 2022 WL 1679114 (¶29) (citing *Smith v. State*, 136 So. 3d 424, 433 (Miss. 2014)).

5. "Something more" that may be used to show authorship includes:
   - the purported sender admits authorship
   - the purported sender is seen composing the communication
   - business records of an internet service provider or cell phone company show that the communication originated from the purported sender's personal computer or cell phone under circumstances in which it is reasonable to believe that only the purported sender would have access to the computer or cell phone
   - the communication contains information that only the purported sender could be expected to know
   - the purported sender responds to an exchange in such a way as to indicate circumstantially that he was in fact the author of the communication
   - **other circumstances peculiar to the particular case may suffice to establish a prima facie showing of authenticity**

6. Once a party makes a prima facie showing of authenticity, the social media evidence is admitted and it goes to the jury, which ultimately determines the evidence's authenticity - - i.e., whether the party alleged actually sent the message. *Webb v. State*, ___ So.3d ____, 2022 WL 1679114 (citing *Young v. Guild*, 7 So. 3d 251, 262 (Miss. 2009)).

7. The judge functions as the *initial gatekeeper* who determines the reliability of the social media evidence by requiring a *prima facie* case for authentication, and the jury then assesses the weight and credibility of the admitted evidence.

      c.   **PRIMA FACIE CASE FOR ADMISSION OF SOCIAL MEDIA:**

1. In *Webb*, the child's mother took the screen shot of the Snapchat messages, but she did not testify at the trial to authenticate the screen shots.

2. The MSSC held that a "screenshot" is the same as a "photograph that has captured what is depicted on a smartphone's screen."

3. There is no requirement that a photograph be authenticated or sponsored by the photographer. Instead, any person with the requisite knowledge of the facts represented in the photograph may authenticate it. *Jackson v. State*, 483 So. 2d 1353, 1355 (Miss. 1986).

4. In *Webb*, the child testified about participating in the communications captured in the screenshots, and that they were a true and accurate depiction of her Snapchat conversations with the defendant.

5. The defendant in *Webb* also asserted that the screen shots were inadmissible based on a "lack of foundation," because the State failed to show it was the defendant, and not some other person, on the other side of these communications.

6. However, the MSSC held that the State need only prove a sufficient prima facie case of authentication, which it did. At that point, the jury—not the trial judge—is tasked with deciding the ultimate weight and worth of the evidence. So the defendant was really attacking the weight of the evidence of the screenshot messages, not their admissibility.

7. "The possibility that someone else may have been using a device goes to the weight of the evidence, not its authenticity." *Garcia v. State*, 300 So. 3d 945, 973 (Miss. 2020).

8. "On issues of witness credibility, the jury determines the weight and credibility of each witness's testimony." *Thomas v. State*, 48 So. 3d 460, 469 (Miss. 2010).

9. In *Webb*, one of the victims testified that she knew it was Webb communicating with her because this his personal account that contained his unique username - - "zwebb30" - - and it was the only account he had ever used to communicate

with her. He also crafted his written communications in the same way he spoke to her. The COA held that this was likely sufficient to prove a *prima facie* case of authenticity.

10. The MSSC held that the mere suggestion that someone else could have accessed a person's social media account does not prevent authentication. That is because the trial judge, as gatekeeper, need not find the evidence is necessarily what the proponent claims - - only that there is sufficient evidence that the jury ultimately might do so. In *Webb*, the Court held that the fact that the messages came from Webb's account, combined with the author's messages and responses, similar conversational tone, and post-screenshot discussions with the mother of one of the victims, was more than sufficient for the jury to make this determination.

RIGHTS BETWEEN COHABITANTS

Today, a significant number of adults forty years of age and younger are cohabiting.

- Thirty percent of Millennials (persons nearing 40) lived in the traditional family (with a spouse and child) in 2019. In contrast, 40% of Gen Xers, 46% of Boomers and 70% of the Silent Generation lived in a traditional family as they approached forty.

- In 2019, 44% of Millennials were married. At that age, 53% of Gen Xers, 61% of Boomers and 81% of Silents were married.

- In 2019, 12% of Millennials were cohabiting with a romantic partner. In contrast, 8% of Gen Xers were cohabiting at the same age. (No comparable data was available for older generations).

https://www.pewresearch.org/social-trends/2020/05/27/as-millennials-near-40-theyre-approaching-family-life-differently-than-previous-generations/

Couples in a long-term committed relationship may share resources, commingle assets and funds, and work as a team, requiring some intervention to sort out financial rights. For the most part, marriage remains the bright-line marker for financial rights between couples. However, courts and legislatures are developing exceptions to address specific financial rights when a cohabiting couple separates.

The Mississippi Supreme Court and Court of Appeals permit recovery by a cohabitant based on agreement, contribution of funds to an asset, or participation in a joint venture or implied partnership. In addition, partners to a void marriage may be entitled to property division, as may cohabitants who were once married.

The Uniform Law Commission recently created a Task Force on the Economic Rights of Cohabitants to draft a proposed uniform law on the topic. Appendix A includes a copy of the act, which allows courts to consider claims by cohabitants based on contribution to the relationship, including contribution of domestic services. The act was adopted by the National Conference of Commissioners on Uniform State Laws in July, 2021.

I. NO RIGHTS BASED SOLELY ON COHABITATION AND HOMEMAKING

The general rule in Mississippi (and most states) is that cohabitants are not entitled to equitable distribution of assets acquired during cohabitation or to any form of spousal support.

Davis v. Davis, 643 So. 2d 931, 936 (Miss. 1994). The Mississippi Supreme Court denied a homemaker cohabitant's request for property division from her partner of thirteen years and the father of her child. She sought an equitable share of $5 million in his name, alleging that she was responsible for homemaking while he was responsible for financial matters. The court held that the assets were not accumulated by their joint efforts and were not divisible upon separation.

Malone v. Odom, 657 So. 2d 1112, 1117 (Miss. 1995). The supreme court held that a chancellor erred in awarding a man's cohabitant an interest in a home titled in his name simply because they had jointly occupied it for many years. The court stated, "[T]he legislature has not extended the rights enjoyed by married people to those who have chosen merely to cohabit or carry on an affair."

II. Rights based on contribution of property or services

A. Financial contribution to asset: Recovery based on unjust enrichment

Cates v. Swain, 215 So. 3d 492, 494 (Miss. 2013). The Mississippi Supreme Court held that a cohabitant may recover against their partner for financial contributions to assets in the other's name, based on unjust enrichment. The chancellor awarded a same-sex cohabitant $44,995 to recoup funds that she invested in her partner's home. The court of appeals reversed, holding that assets may not be divided between cohabitants based on implied contractual remedies. The supreme court reversed the court of appeals, holding that a cohabitant may recover against her partner based on unjust enrichment when "the person sought to be charged is in possession of money or property which in good conscience and justice he should not retain but should deliver to another." *See also Carlson v. Brabham,* 199 So. 3d 735, 744 (Miss. Ct. App. 2016) (recognizing doctrine but finding no basis for unjust enrichment).

B. Participation in joint venture or implied partnership

Carlson v. Brabham, 199 So. 3d 735, 740-43 (Miss. Ct. App. 2016). In a 2016 case, the court of appeals discussed implied partnership and joint venture as theories of recovery for cohabitants but found that the petitioner failed to meet the elements of either. A woman claimed that she and her cohabitant entered an implied partnership regarding his business and that they entered a joint venture to acquire, renovate, and sell houses.

To establish an implied partnership, a plaintiff must prove (1) the intent to form a partnership; (2) that the cohabitant had some control of the business; and, most importantly, (3) profit sharing. She failed to present proof of any of the three. She encouraged her partner to incorporate his business, was listed as the secretary and treasurer after incorporation, and was paid as a part-time bookkeeper. He was consistently listed as the sole owner and received all distributions. The company operated in the same manner as it did before their relationship, except that she provided paid bookkeeping services. The fact that he used income from the business to pay for some of their expenses did not mean that she shared in company profits.

Nor did she prove a joint venture with respect to two houses in his name. During their relationship, he built a home on land that he owned, funding construction from his company's checking account. He performed much of the work and made the mortgage payments, while she provided some minor labor. There was no proof of an agreement to enter a joint venture and no proof that the purpose was to generate profit.

C. Financial contribution to household expenses: No recovery

Nichols v. Funderburk, 881 So. 2d 266, 271 (Miss. Ct. App. 2003), *affirmed,* 883 So. 2d 554 (Miss. 2004). A woman who cohabited with her partner and the father of her children for fourteen years was not entitled to division of assets acquired by her partner, though she managed a restaurant owned by him and contributed her income to household expenses. The decision appears to be based in part on the fact that she was paid $240 a week for her services in the restaurant. The court rejected her argument that she was entitled to a constructive trust on the home titled in his name because she contributed financially by paying utility bills and making improvements to the home (purchasing paint and flooring).

Potential argument: It could be argued that when one cohabitant builds equity with payments, while the other pays fungible costs such as food, childcare, utilities, or other household expenses, the equity-building spouse has been unjustly enriched to the extent they have been relieved of the obligation to make those payments. The Indiana Court of Appeals affirmed an award of $18,000 to a former cohabitant, finding that her partner was unjustly enriched – she performed all of the home-making and childcare duties, including caring for his child by another woman – while he built his business. *Turner v. Freed,* 792 N.E.2d 947, 948 (Ind. Ct. App. 2003). The Wisconsin Supreme Court affirmed an unjust enrichment award of $113,090, holding that there was sufficient evidence that the plaintiff's homemaking services and assistance in her partner's business "fertilized the increased value of Watts' property, not only by helping him in the business but also by freeing him from many nonbusiness tasks." *Watts v. Watts,* 448 N.W.2d 292 (Wis. Ct. App. 1989) (*Watts II*) (considering appeal after remand); *see also Watts v. Watts,* 405 N.W.2d 303, 305 (Wis. 1987) (*Watts I*) (considering an appeal from the grant of a motion to dismiss for failure to state a claim).

III. Rights based on express agreement

Williams v. Mason, 556 So. 2d 1045, 1049 (Miss. 1990). The Mississippi Supreme Court held that a woman was entitled to a quantum meruit recovery from her cohabitant's estate – she provided homemaking services for him for twenty-four years based on his promise that she would receive his property at his death. The court stated, "when one has provided services for the other in reasonable reliance upon a promise . . . the promisee may recover of and from the estate on a quantum meruit basis."

In re Estate of Reaves, 744 So. 2d 799, 802 (Miss. Ct. App. 1999). The supreme court also enforced an agreement between a same-sex couple for financial payments upon their separation. The court rejected the argument that the agreement was unenforceable as against public policy, stating, "No authority states that a contract between two unmarried persons is illegal. . . . the law of this State does not support any finding of illegality with regard to this contract."

IV. Rights based on the putative spouse doctrine

The putative spouse doctrine is usually applied to grant property division to a person who in good faith believed themselves to be married. The Mississippi Court of Appeals has expanded the doctrine to apply to all void marriages.

Chrismond v. Chrismond, 52 So. 2d 624, 630 (Miss. 1951). In 1951, the Mississippi Supreme Court affirmed an award of assets to a woman who married in good faith, unaware that her husband was already married. The court noted that she had worked long hours to help build his business and that assets titled in his name had been accumulated by their joint efforts. The decision also appears to hold that in Mississippi, a putative spouse is not entitled to alimony, which must be based on a valid marriage.

Cotton v. Cotton, 44 So. 3d 371, 375 (Miss. Ct. App. 2010). The Mississippi Court of Appeals held that the putative spouse doctrine does not require a good faith belief that a marriage is valid. A wife of thirty-seven years who was a homemaker and cared for the couple's four children was entitled to equitable distribution of assets even though her marriage was annulled as bigamous. She had never divorced her first husband. The court emphasized that her efforts as a homemaker assisted her partner's acquisition of assets: "Fannie's domestic efforts enabled, or at least assisted in allowing, Eddie to work outside the home as the primary breadwinner."

V. EXCEPTION: RIGHTS BETWEEN ONCE-MARRIED COHABITANTS

A. Equitable distribution

Pickens v. Pickens, 490 So. 2d 872, 875 (Miss. 1986). When a formerly married couple resumed cohabitation for twenty years after their divorce, the supreme court held that division of assets was proper, stating that "our law authorizes and sanctions an equitable division of property accumulated by two persons as a result of their joint efforts. This would be the case were a common law business partnership breaking up. It is equally the case where a man and woman, who have accumulated property in the course of a non-marital cohabitation, permanently separate." The court went on to emphasize that nonfinancial contributions should be considered: "[W]here one party to the relationship acts without compensation to perform work or render services to a business enterprise or performs work or services generally regarded as domestic in nature, these are nevertheless economic contributions." The language of the opinion appears to encompass all cohabitants. However, later decisions limited the holding to formerly married cohabitants or couples who entered an invalid marriage. *See Davis v. Davis,* 643 So. 2d 931, 936 (Miss. 1994) (emphasizing that the woman, Elvis, had a chance to marry her millionaire cohabitant and turned him down); *Nichols v. Funderburk,* 881 So. 2d 266, 271 (Miss. Ct. App. 2003), *affirmed,* 883 So. 2d 554 (Miss. 2004).

Bunyard v. Bunyard, 828 So. 2d 775, 778 (Miss. 2002) (also based on commingling). A divorcing wife was awarded a portion of assets acquired in her husband's name during their premarital cohabitation, based in part on their joint efforts. The supreme court held that it was appropriate to divide some assets acquired prior to marriage because the chancellor recognized "a period of cohabitation which involved joint efforts to accumulate assets, followed by a valid marriage where the same joint efforts continued."

B. Reimbursement for domestic services

Woolridge v. Woolridge, 856 So. 2d 446, 452 (Miss. Ct. App. 2003). The court of appeals articulated a new theory for recovery by a formerly married homemaker cohabitant in 2003. The court held that a woman who lived with her ex-husband for eleven years after their divorce was entitled to reimbursement for her domestic services. The court relied on dicta from earlier cases stating that domestic services are economic contributions to the accumulation of assets. The court affirmed the chancellor's award compensating the woman for the market value of her services as a caregiver. The court rejected her former husband's argument that the award amounted to "palimony": "Steve and Debra were more than 'pals' by virtue of their previous marriage, their having a second child during their post-divorce period of cohabitation, their holding themselves out to the public as being husband and wife . . . . But for want of obtaining another marriage license, they lived in the same relationship in which they had lived from 1973 through 1994."

VI. JOINTLY OWNED PROPERTY

Jones v. Graphia, 95 So. 3d 751, 755 (Miss. Ct. App. 2012). In a 2012 case, the court of appeals held that the joint title presumption has been abrogated in Mississippi. An unmarried couple took title to a home together as joint tenants with rights of survivorship. When they separated, the man, who contributed the entire purchase price, was awarded the property in a partition action. The court of appeals rejected his partner's argument that joint titling of property created a presumption that her partner intended a gift of one half of the property to her. Additionally, the court held that when one owner files for partition, the court may adjust the equities between the parties under the partition statutes. Four judges dissented, asserting that the "equity adjustment" permitted by the statute relates to payment of expenses during the joint ownership, not to payments made before formation of the joint ownership. *Id.* For a similar approach, see *Beale v. Beale,* 577 P. 2d 507, 510 (Or. 1972) (holding that jointly titled home should be divided based on the parties' intent and not by general rules of co-tenancy). See MISS. CODE ANN. § 11-21-33.

VII. ALIMONY

Pickens v. Pickens, 490 So. 2d 872, 875 (Miss. 1986). The Mississippi Supreme Court has stated that alimony is available only upon proof of a valid marriage. In one case that seems to stand alone, the supreme court upheld an award of thirty-six months of payments to a woman in ill health when her husband under a void marriage left her. The court noted that the case was unusual and that the woman would otherwise be destitute. *Taylor v. Taylor,* 317 So. 2d 422, 423 (Miss. 1975). The court of appeals later characterized the *Taylor* order as a division of property *See Pickens v. Pickens,* 490 So. 2d 872, 875 (Miss. 1986); *Cotton v. Cotton,* 44 So. 3d 371, 377 (Miss. Ct. App. 2010).

VIII. GOVERNMENT AND EMPLOYMENT BENEFITS

A few states have extended other benefits to cohabitants. For example, in a few states, cohabitants may receive workers' compensation benefits. To date, no Mississippi case has recognized benefits other than division of assets as described above. The Mississippi Supreme Court reversed a chancellor's grant of a life estate in homestead to a woman who lived with the owner for more than thirty years. In the absence of an agreement that she would be compensated for her care of him, equity could not provide a remedy. *In re Estate of Alexander,* 445 So. 2d 836, 840 (Miss. 1984) (provision of relief a matter for legislative, not judicial action). The supreme court has also rejected the claim of an unmarried cohabitant seeking workers' compensation benefits as a dependent widow. *Dale Polk Constr. Co. v. White,* 287 So. 2d 278, 280 (Miss. 1973).

For purposes of entitlement to Social Security benefits, federal law defines a spouse to include a putative spouse – one who entered into a marriage in good faith without knowledge of impediments to the marriage. 42 U.S.C. § 416(h)(1)(B).

Uniform Cohabitants' Economic Remedies Act

drafted by the

NATIONAL CONFERENCE OF COMMISSIONERS
ON UNIFORM STATE LAWS

and by it

APPROVED AND RECOMMENDED FOR ENACTMENT
IN ALL THE STATES

at its

ANNUAL CONFERENCE
MEETING IN ITS ONE-HUNDRED-AND-THIRTIETH YEAR
MADISON, WISCONSIN
JULY 10–15, 2021

WITHOUT PREFATORY NOTE AND COMMENTS

May 4, 2022

Uniform Cohabitants' Economic Remedies Act

Section 1. Title

This [act] may be cited as the Uniform Cohabitants' Economic Remedies Act.

Section 2. Definitions

In this [act]:

(1) "Cohabitant" means each of two individuals not married to each other who live together as a couple after each has reached the age of majority or been emancipated. The term does not include individuals who are too closely related to marry each other legally.

(2) "Cohabitants' agreement" means an agreement between two individuals concerning contributions to the relationship if the individuals are to become, are, or were cohabitants. The term includes a waiver of rights under this [act].

(3) "Contributions to the relationship" means contributions of a cohabitant that benefit the other cohabitant, both cohabitants, or the cohabitants' relationship, in the form of efforts, activities, services, or property. The term:

(A) includes:

(i) cooking, cleaning, shopping, household maintenance, conducting errands, and other domestic services for the benefit of the other cohabitant or the cohabitants' relationship; and

(ii) otherwise caring for the other cohabitant, a child in common, or another family member of the other cohabitant; and

(B) does not include sexual relations.

(4) "Property" means anything that may be the subject of ownership, whether real or personal, tangible or intangible, legal or equitable, or any interest therein. The term includes

responsibility for a debt.

(5) "Record" means information:

(A) inscribed on a tangible medium; or

(B) stored in an electronic or other medium and retrievable in perceivable form.

(6) "State" means a state of the United States, the District of Columbia, Puerto Rico, the United States Virgin Islands, or any other territory or possession subject to the jurisdiction of the United States.

(7) "Termination of cohabitation" means the earliest of:

(A) the death of a cohabitant;

(B) the date the cohabitants stop living together as a couple; or

(C) the date of the cohabitants' marriage to each other.

Section 3. Scope

This [act] applies only to a contractual or equitable claim between cohabitants concerning an interest, promise, or obligation arising from contributions to the relationship. The rights and remedies of cohabitants under this [act] are not exclusive.

Section 4. Right of Cohabitant to Bring Action

(a) An individual who is or was a cohabitant may commence an action on a contractual or equitable claim that arises out of contributions to the relationship. The action is not:

(1) barred because of a sexual relationship between the cohabitants;

(2) subject to additional substantive or procedural requirements because the parties to the action are or were cohabitants or because of a sexual relationship between the cohabitants; or

(3) extinguished by the marriage of the cohabitants to each other.

(b) The action may be commenced on behalf of a deceased cohabitant's estate.

(c) The action may be commenced against a deceased cohabitant's estate and adjudicated under law of this state applicable to a claim against a decedent's estate.

Section 5. Governing Law

(a) Except as otherwise provided in this [act], a claim under this [act] is governed by other law of this state, including this state's choice-of-law rules.

(b) The validity, enforceability, interpretation, and construction of a cohabitants' agreement are determined by:

(1) the law of the state designated in the agreement if the designation is valid under other law of this state; or

(2) in the absence of a designation effective under paragraph (1), the law of this state, including this state's choice-of-law rules.

Section 6. Cohabitants' Agreement

(a) A cohabitants' agreement may be oral, in a record, express, or implied-in-fact.

(b) Contributions to the relationship are sufficient consideration for a cohabitants' agreement.

(c) A claim for breach of a cohabitants' agreement accrues on breach and may be commenced, subject to [cite to the applicable statute of limitations on contractual claims], during cohabitation or after termination of cohabitation.

(d) A term in a cohabitants' agreement that affects adversely a child's right to support is unenforceable.

(e) A term in a cohabitants' agreement that requires or limits the ability of a cohabitant to pursue a civil, criminal, or administrative remedy is voidable to the extent the remedy is available because the cohabitant is a victim of a [crime of violence].

Legislative Note: *Subsection (e) should refer to a state's statutory or judicial definition of "crime of violence" or, in absence of a definition, cite to appropriate crimes.*

Section 7. Equitable Relief

(a) Unless maintaining the action is inconsistent with a valid cohabitants' agreement, a cohabitant may commence an equitable action against the other cohabitant concerning entitlement to property based on contributions to the relationship. The action is in addition to any remedy otherwise available to the cohabitant under this [act] or other law.

(b) An equitable claim based on contributions to the relationship accrues on termination of cohabitation and is subject to equitable defenses.

(c) In addition to other law governing an equitable claim, the court adjudicating a claim under this section shall consider:

(1) the nature and value of contributions to the relationship by each cohabitant, including the value to each cohabitant and the market value of the contributions;

(2) the duration and continuity of the cohabitation;

(3) the extent to which a cohabitant reasonably relied on representations or conduct of the other cohabitant;

(4) the extent to which a cohabitant demonstrated an intent to share, or not to share, property with the other cohabitant; and

(5) other relevant factors.

Section 8. Effect of Court Order or Judgment on Third Party

(a) [Except as provided in subsection (c), a][A] court order or judgment granting relief under this [act] against a cohabitant or a cohabitant's estate is an order or judgment in favor of a general creditor.

(b) A court order or judgment granting relief under this [act] may not impair the rights of a good-faith purchaser from, or secured creditor of, a cohabitant.

[Alternative A

(c) A court order or judgment granting relief under this [act] may not impair the right or interest of a cohabitant's [spouse] or surviving [spouse] to the cohabitant's property.

Alternative B

(c) A court order or judgment granting relief under this [act] may not impair the right or interest of a cohabitant's [spouse] or surviving [spouse] to the cohabitant's property unless:

(1) the [spouse] had notice of the proceedings on the claim and an opportunity to be heard;

(2) before entering the order or judgment, the court determines based on the totality of the circumstances that justice requires that all or part of the cohabitant's claim should be satisfied; and

(3) the order or judgment preserves as much of the [spouse's] right or interest as appropriate or legally required.

Alternative C

(c) A court order or judgment granting relief based on an equitable claim under Section 7 may not impair the right or interest of a cohabitant's [spouse] or surviving [spouse] to the cohabitant's property.

Alternative D

(c) A court order or judgment granting relief based on an equitable claim under Section 7 may not impair the right or interest of a cohabitant's [spouse] or surviving [spouse] to the cohabitant's property unless:

(1) the [spouse] had notice of the proceedings on the claim and an opportunity to be heard;

(2) before entering the order or judgment, the court determines based on the totality of the circumstances that justice requires that all or part of the cohabitant's claim should be satisfied; and

(3) the order or judgment preserves as much of the [spouse's] right or interest as appropriate or legally required.

End of Alternatives]

Legislative Note: This section provides five options for treating a claim of a spouse and a cohabitant to a married cohabitant's property:

(1) A state that chooses to treat a cohabitant's claim as a general creditor's claim in all cases should adopt only subsections (a) and (b) and not adopt any of the alternatives for subsection (c).

(2) A state that chooses to insulate a spouse from both contractual and equitable claims of a cohabitant should adopt Alternative A.

(3) A state that chooses to insulate a spouse from both contractual and equitable claims of a cohabitant but allow a court under certain circumstances to find that justice requires at least some satisfaction of the cohabitant's claim against a married cohabitant should adopt Alternative B.

(4) A state that chooses to treat a cohabitant's contractual claim as a general creditor's claim and insulate a spouse only from an equitable claim under Section 7 should adopt Alternative C.

(5) A state that chooses to treat a cohabitant's contractual claim as a general creditor's claim and allow a court under certain circumstances to find that justice requires some satisfaction of the cohabitant's equitable claim under Section 7 against a married cohabitant should adopt Alternative D.

If a state's law provides that individuals in a civil union or domestic partnership have a right comparable to individuals in a marriage, the state should insert the appropriate terms in addition to "spouse".

Section 9. Principles of Law and Equity

The principles of law and equity supplement this [act] except to the extent inconsistent with this [act].

Section 10. Uniformity of Application and Construction

In applying and construing this uniform act, a court shall consider the promotion of uniformity of the law among jurisdictions that enact it.

Section 11. Relation to Electronic Signatures in Global and National Commerce Act

This [act] modifies, limits, or supersedes the Electronic Signatures in Global and National Commerce Act, 15 U.S.C. Section 7001 et seq.[, as amended], but does not modify, limit, or supersede 15 U.S.C. Section 7001(c), or authorize electronic delivery of any of the notices described in 15 U.S.C. Section 7003(b).

Legislative Note: It is the intent of this act to incorporate future amendments to the cited federal law. A state in which the constitution or other law does not permit incorporation of future amendments when a federal statute is incorporated into state law should omit the phrase ", as amended". A state in which, in the absence of a legislative declaration, future amendments are incorporated into state law also should omit the phrase.

Section 12. Transitional Provisions

(a) This [act] applies to a cohabitants' agreement made [before,] on[,] or after [the effective date of this [act]].

(b) This [act] applies to an equitable claim under this [act] that accrues [before,] on[,] or after [the effective date of this [act]].

Legislative Note: A state that previously has not recognized a claim between cohabitants based on contract or in equity arising from contributions to their relationship may choose to apply this act only to a claim that accrues on or after the effective date.

[Section 13. Severability

If a provision of this [act] or its application to a person or circumstance is held invalid, the invalidity does not affect another provision or application that can be given effect without the invalid provision.]

Legislative Note: Include this section only if the state lacks a general severability statute or a decision by the highest court of the state adopting a general rule of severability.

[Section 14. Repeals; Conforming Amendments

(a) . . .

(b) . . .]

Legislative Note: A state should examine its statutes to determine whether repeals or conforming revisions are required by provisions of this act relating to accrual of an equitable claim. See Section 7(b). A state also should consider whether modification to other law is desirable to reflect the state's public policy regarding domestic partnerships or civil unions.

Section 15. Effective Date

This [act] takes effect . . .

PARENT RELOCATION: THE MISSISSIPPI RULE

I. RELOCATION IS NOT A MATERIAL CHANGE IN CIRCUMSTANCES.

Mississippi is in a minority of states in which a custodial parent's move, in and of itself, is not a material change that adversely affects a child. Something more than the mere fact of relocation must be shown to trigger an *Albright* best interests analysis.

The fact that the move negatively impacts the relationship between the child and the noncustodial parent is not considered a material change. In *Holland v. Spain*, 483 So. 2d 318, 321 (Miss. 1986) the Mississippi Supreme Court stated, "We regard as legally irrelevant to the matter of permanent custody the fact that taking the children to a distant state effectively curtails the noncustodial parent's visitation rights."

- *Robertson v. Roberts,* 95 So. 3d 727, 729-30 (Miss. Ct. App. 2012) (mother's proposed move to New Mexico with her serviceman husband was not a basis for modification of custody) (fact that the move would end mid-week visitation was "legally irrelevant").

- A mother's move from Hattiesburg to Batesville three months after divorce was not a material change in circumstances; the fact that the father's mid-week visitation was difficult did not justify modification. *Lambert v. Lambert*, 872 So. 2d 679, 686 (Miss. Ct. App. 2003) (child's anxiety was caused by divorce and subsequent modification litigation rather than relocation).

- In a modification action based on a custodial mother's move to California, the court of appeals stated that a distant move is material, but not necessarily an adverse change, even if the noncustodial parent's visitation rights are curtailed as a result of the move. *Balius v. Gaines,* 908 So. 2d 791, 801-02 (Miss. Ct. App. 2005).

- The supreme court made a similar statement in a case in which a custodial father was transferred to Hawaii for military service: "[W]here one spouse has custody of children under a divorce decree and their employment or livelihood requires that they move or be transferred to another state of this nation, this does not constitute a change in circumstances which would adversely affect the children, under ordinary conditions, even though it might cause a hardship on the other spouse with regard to existing visitation privileges. The fact that Hawaii or Alaska happens to be the state of transfer is of no consequence." *Pearson v. Pearson,* 458 So. 2d 711, 714 (Miss. 1984).

- When a custodial mother moved to Houston, Texas to seek employment, the court rejected the father's appeal for modification, stating, "Surely, it must be the law that such a change of residence by the person having custody is not a material change in circumstances which would justify a reconsideration of an order for primary custody." *Cheek v. Ricker*, 431 So. 2d 1139, 1144 (Miss. 1983).

In a 2021 case, the court of appeals declined to address a father's request that the court revise the relocation rule, noting that the rule was long-established and should be addressed by the supreme court, not the court of appeals. The parents of two children divorced in 2014, agreeing to joint legal custody, physical custody in the mother, and extensive visitation for the father. Two years later, their daughter was diagnosed with dyslexia and Expressive/Receptive Language Disorder. The parents agreed that the mother would move to Memphis to enroll her in a school for children with dyslexia beginning in January 2017. In April of 2018, the mother decided to enroll the daughter in the Currey-Ingram School in Nashville, a move that the father objected to as unnecessary, disruptive to his relationship with his daughter, and too expensive. The chancellor found that the mother's relocation from Memphis to Nashville was a not a material change in circumstances that warranted modification of custody to the father. However, he did find that it required modification of the father's visitation. The father was granted five weeks in the summer, two long visits each semester, alternating spring breaks, alternating holidays, and the option to visit his daughter in Nashville one weekend a month. The court of appeals rejected the father's request that the court revisit the Mississippi rule that a custodial parent's relocation is not, in itself, a material change in circumstances. *Smith v. Smith,* 318 So. 3d 484 (Miss. Ct. App. 2021).

II. A MOVE BY A JOINT PHYSICAL CUSTODIAN IS A MATERIAL CHANGE IN CIRCUMSTANCES.

In contrast, a move by one joint physical custodian will almost always be a material change in circumstances warranting a change to sole physical custody in one parent. As the court of appeals noted, a "shared custody agreement between parents of a child of school age, living in two different states, would be quite difficult to maintain." *See Lackey v. Fuller,* 755 So. 2d 1083, 1088-89 (Miss. 2000) (mother's move to New York made exchange of custody every two weeks impractical); *Sobieske v. Preslar,* 755 So. 2d 410, 413 (Miss. 2000) (joint custody modified when mother decided to move to Atlanta); *McRree v. McRree,* 723 So. 2d 1217, 1219-20 (Miss. Ct. App. 1998) (mother's move to Texas made alternating joint custody impractical). In contrast to moves by a sole physical custodian, a joint custodial parent's relocation often results in modification to the non-relocating parent. When a joint custodial parent moves, the move is a material change in circumstances because it almost always makes the exercise of joint custody impractical. Under the *Albright* analysis, the parent who remains behind may be favored on stability of the home environment, stability of employment, the child's home, school, and community record, and the presence of extended family in the area.

- The court of appeals affirmed a chancellor's modification from joint physical custody to sole custody in the father when the mother moved eighty miles away. The move required weekly transfers of the four-year-old girl. *Pearson v. Pearson,* 11 So. 3d 178, 182 (Miss. Ct. App. 2009) (father favored on mental health).

- A joint custodial mother's planned move from Jackson to Memphis was a material change in circumstances warranting transfer of custody to the father, who remained in Jackson. *Porter v. Porter*, 23 So. 3d 438, 448 (Miss. 2009) (finding for father on children's home, school, and community record and stability of home environment and stability of employment).

- A court properly granted a father sole physical and legal custody when the joint custodial mother moved from Mississippi to Arizona without consulting him. *Elliott v. Elliott,* 877 So. 2d 450, 455-56 (Miss. Ct. App. 2003).

- An agreement requiring weekly shared custody was modified when parents moved to different locations. The court awarded custody to the father, based in part on the oldest child's preference to live with him. *See Massey v. Huggins,* 799 So. 2d 902, 906 (Miss. Ct. App. 2001) (joint custody requiring four weekly exchanges impractical).

- A joint custodial mother's decision to move to Houston was a material change making joint custody impossible. The chancellor awarded custody to the father who remained in Mississippi. *McRree v. McRree,* 723 So. 2d 1217, 1220 (Miss. Ct. App. 1998).

Only one case was found in which a relocating joint custodial parent was awarded custody. A joint custodial father's move from north Mississippi to Memphis was a material change requiring modification. The court awarded him sole custody because he was better able to provide childcare and had greater job stability. *Rinehart v. Barnes,* 819 So. 2d 564, 565-66 (Miss. Ct. App. 2002).

III.   EXTENSIVE VISITATION TO THE NONCUSTODIAL PARENT DOES NOT ALTER THE RULE.

In a 1986 case, a father with extensive visitation (six out of every fourteen days) sought unsuccessfully to enforce a relocation provision in the couple's divorce agreement. The parents agreed to divided custody of their three children, with the father having custody of the older son and the mother custody of their daughter and young son. Their agreement stated that, with regard to the two older children, a move by one parent would be considered a material change in circumstances requiring a hearing and approval by the chancery court. It also provided that the older children should have an opportunity to state their preference for consideration by the court. When the mother decided to move from Union County to Hinds County, the father sought to enforce the provision. The chancellor held that the mother's move was not a material change in circumstances, but that their agreement amounted to de facto joint custody, since the father had extensive visitation. Because the move would make joint custody impossible, the chancellor modified custody of the girl to her father. The supreme court reversed, holding that the agreement was not tantamount to joint custody. And, sole custody could not be modified without a material change in circumstances, which did not occur. *Rutledge v. Rutledge,* 487 So. 2d 218, 220 (Miss. 1986).

However, in two cases where the children spent *more* time with the noncustodial parent than the custodial parent, courts modified custody in part based on that fact. *Robinson v. Brown,* 58 So. 3d 38, 43-44 (Miss. Ct. App. 2011); *Self v. Lewis,* 64 So. 3d 578, 586 (Miss. Ct. App. 2011). In *Self,* the chancellor found that the parents had a de facto joint custody arrangement. The court of appeals disagreed – the agreement stated that the father had physical custody – but affirmed based on a material change in circumstances.

IV. AGREEMENTS TO ALTER THE MISSISSIPPI RULE ARE UNENFORCEABLE.

A. Agreement that children will remain in a certain location

In *Bell v. Bell,* 572 So. 2d 841, 845-46 (Miss. 1990), a father sought enforcement of a divorce agreement that provided: "[N]either the husband nor the wife shall remove the children from the jurisdiction without the express written consent of the other. It being the mutual intent of both parties that the children live in the Tupelo area." The mother planned to move to Jackson with their two boys, hoping to find better employment opportunities. The chancellor modified custody of the older boy to his father. The Mississippi Supreme Court reversed, holding that the provision was void as against public policy and unenforceable. The court recognized that one's "social, economic, professional and educational advancement frequently dictate to reasonable persons that they move from one community to another. " *Id.* (also noting the constitutional right to travel). The court held that a chancellor may not order, and parents may not agree, that children will remain in a particular location for their entire minority. The court went further to state that a custodial parent's move "is certainly not *per se* a material change of circumstances" – determining a child's residence is an incident of custody and in the discretion of the custodial parent. *Id.* at 847.

B. Agreement that custody transfers upon relocation by the custodial parent

The supreme court held invalid an agreement that upon a custodial parent's relocation, custody automatically transferred to the noncustodial parent. In *McManus v. Howard*, 569 So. 2d 1213, 1216 (Miss. 1990), the parents of two boys agreed that the mother would have physical custody but that if she moved from Columbus, Mississippi, custody would transfer to the father. When the mother planned to remarry, she sought a declaratory judgment that the provisions were unenforceable. The chancellor denied her motion and confirmed a transfer of custody of one of their two children to the father. The court, citing *Bell,* held that a chancellor is charged with determining the custody that is in children's best interests. Parties cannot agree to future custody arrangements that deprive a chancellor of that authority.

C. Agreement that a move is a material change in circumstances

The Mississippi appellate courts have not directly addressed whether parents may agree that relocation will constitute a material change triggering a best interest analysis. However, the decision in *Rutledge, supra*, seems to be based on that premise. The parents agreed that relocation would be a material change. The court found that there was no material change and the supreme court affirmed.

V. To modify custody upon relocation, a noncustodial parent must proof adverse circumstances other than relocation.

The Mississippi Supreme Court has recognized, however that a move may be one of several circumstances that, together, constitute a material adverse change – considering "the totality of the circumstances." In most cases in which relocation resulted in modification, the noncustodial parent was able to point to adverse changes in addition to relocation.

- *Munday v. McClendon,* 287 So. 3d 303 (Miss. Ct. App. 2019) (mother's lack of attention to child's medical needs; child was cared for by relative with substance abuse issues; mother kept child from father; multiple school absences; moved away from extended family).

- *Bennett v. Bennett,* 242 So. 3d 210, 213 (Miss. Ct. App. 2018) (custodial mother's decision to move to St. Louis was a material change in circumstances; modifying to sole custody in father; mother did not have a permanent home or employment; was engaged to someone in St. Louis but with no marriage plans).

- *Robinson v. Brown*, 58 So. 3d 38, 43-44 (Miss. Ct. App. 2011) (based on mother's relocation, fact that child was more bonded to father and had spent more time with him than custodial mother; child had deteriorated relationship with mother; separation from older sister would negatively impact her) (" the impact of a relocation of the custodial parent upon the child constitutes a factor that the chancellor permissibly considers on the motion for modification").

- *Self v. Lewis,* 64 So. 3d 578, 586 (Miss. Ct. App. 2011) (custodial father had multiple women stay with him, including an eighteen-year-old; mother had cared for girls more than father and was more involved in their activities; father was involved in questionable business activities; father's proposed move to Florida).

- *Stark v. Anderson,* 748 So. 2d 838, 843 (Miss. Ct. App. 1999) (custodial mother's frequent moves, cohabitation, inappropriate discipline, relocation to Colorado, stepfather drank excessively and child feared him; mother's mental health issues; failure to provide adequate medical care).

- *Stevison v. Woods,* 560 So. 2d 176, 180 (Miss. 1990) (modification of split custody after mother's move to Alaska with her daughter; the move separated the girl from her brother, with whom she visited every day in Mississippi; mother's relationship with her son was strained).

In several cases, a child's stated preference to remain with the non-relocating parent has been an important factor in granting modification.

- *Connelly v. Lammey,* 982 So. 2d 997, 999-1000 (Miss. Ct. App. 2008) (modification after mother's move to Nevada; based on child's preference, removal from extended family, and mother's poor handling of move).

- *Marter v. Marter*, 914 So. 2d 743, 749-50 (Miss. Ct. App. 2005) (custody modified to father after mother's relocation to Nashville; thirteen-year-old daughter was regularly left alone there; she wanted to move back with father; she had extended family in Mississippi, including close female relatives; her grades had dropped after the move; expert witness said she was adversely affected by the move).

A parent's lack of good faith in negotiating custody may lead to modification based on relocation. Custody was properly transferred to a father based on evidence that the custodial mother agreed to provide the father with mid-week visitation and every other weekend, even though she planned to move 500 miles away immediately after divorce, making the visitation agreement impossible. The court of appeals affirmed the chancellor's modification of custody based on a material change in circumstances. *Pulliam v. Smith,* 872 So. 2d 790, 794-95 (Miss. Ct. App. 2004) (chancellor based ruling on fraud on the court).

VI. Trends: Other states

Today, most states have moved away from the notion that a custodial parent's relocation is not a material change in circumstances. Some states legislatures have adopted a multi-factor test that examines the custodial parent's good faith, the impact on visitation, the noncustodial parent's good faith in contesting the move, and the child's best interests. In other states, relocation is considered under the judicially created material change of circumstances test and triggers a best interests analysis.

A. Statutory factor-based tests

The Alabama, Florida, Louisiana, and Tennessee legislature have enacted statutes addressing relocation, which

- Require a relocating parent to notify the other a specified period (between 45 and 60 days) before a move;
- Provide for a court hearing if the non-relocating parent objects; and
- Instruct courts to consider specific factors in determining whether custody should be modified in light of relocation.
- Examples of factors include

(1) the extent and duration of the child's relationship with each parent and with siblings;
(2) the child's age and development and the impact of the move on the child;
(3) whether the relationship with the non-relocating parent can be preserved through visitation;
(4) the preference of a child of twelve or older;
(4) whether the relocating parent has a pattern of supporting or thwarting the other's relationship with the child;
(5) the parents' reasons for proposing or opposing the move; and
(6) whether the move will enhance the parent and child's quality of life.

Alabama (2003) is one of the few states that has a presumption that relocation is NOT in a child's best interests. In the absence of domestic violence or child abuse, there is a rebuttable presumption that it is not in the child's best interest to relocate. ALA. CODE δ 30-3-169.4.

Florida (2009). The statute provides that there is no presumption in favor of or against relocation; however, it places the burden of proof on the relocating parent to prove by a preponderance of the evidence that the move is in the child's best interests. FLA. STAT. ANN. 61.13001.

Louisiana (2012). The parent proposing relocation has the burden of proving that relocation is in good faith and in the child's best interests. LA. REV. STAT. 9:355.10. The Act also provides that the petition must be set for hearing within sixty days of filing. LA. REV. STAT. 9:355.13.

Tennessee (2018). TENN. CODE ANN. δ 36-6-108 (2018). The Tennessee statute does not include a presumption in favor of or against relocation and provides judges with considerable discretion to determine what arrangement is in the child's best interest. *Franklin v. Franklin,* 2021 WL 5500722

(Tenn. Ct. App. Nov. 24, 2021) (affirming trial court's denial of father's motion to modify custody based on mother's move to Houston; child was more closely bonded to mother and her family; move would enhance mother and child's quality of life). *See also Dungey v. Dungey,* 2020 WL 5666906 (Tenn. Ct. App. Sept. 23, 2020) (affirming trial court's modification of custody of thirteen-year-old boy to father when mother moved to Germany; based on boy's close relationship with father's family and his stated preference to live with his father; move would enhance mother's life but not son's); *Shaeffer v. Patterson,* 2019 WL 6824903 (Tenn. Ct. App. Dec. 13, 2019) (affirming trial court's refusal to modify custody when mother moved 94 miles from father's home where she had large extended family; father's visitation not affected by move).

B. Judicially created factor-based tests

In some states, courts have enumerated factors for courts to follow in applying the material change of circumstances test to relocation.

South Carolina. Prior to 2004, South Carolina courts applied a presumption that relocation was not in a child's best interest. The South Carolina Supreme Court overruled that line of cases in *Latimer v. Farmer,* 602 S.E. 2d 32 (S.C. 2004), holding instead that a parent seeking modification must prove that there has been a substantial change in circumstances that affecting the child's welfare and that modification is in the child's best interest. *Id.* at 35. The court held that relocation is not a per se material change in circumstances – it is a factor to be considered by the court. The court listed factors considered by other states, without specifically adopting them, including the reasons for the move, the impact on the child's relationships, the closeness of the child to parents, whether the move would improve the quality of life for the custodial parent and child, and the feasibility of alternative visitation arrangements that would preserve the noncustodial parent-child relationship.

Arkansas. In Arkansas, a custodial parent's relocation is not in itself a material change in circumstances. Interestingly, prior to 2003, Arkansas law provided a factor-based test for determining custody upon relocation. In *Hollandsworth v. Knyzewski,* 109 S.W. 3d 653(Ark. 2003), the Arkansas Supreme Court overruled prior cases and held that "relocation of a primary custodian and his or her children alone is not a material change in circumstance. We announce a presumption in favor of relocation for custodial parents with primary custody." A noncustodial parent must prove that the relocation constitutes a material change and that it is in the child's best interest to modify custody, considering the following factors: "(1) the reason for the relocation; (2) the educational, health, and leisure opportunities available in the location in which the custodial parent and children will relocate; (3) visitation and communication schedule for the noncustodial parent; (4) the effect of the move on the extended family relationships in the location in which the custodial parent and children will relocate, as well as Arkansas; and, (5) preference of the child, including the age, maturity, and the reasons given by the child as to his or her preference." *Id.* at 664. In 2017, the Arkansas Supreme Court acknowledged that most states now apply a best-interest test to determine custody upon relocation. The court reaffirmed the *Hollandsworth* rule but limited it to cases in which the parents have a traditional visitation schedule, with the noncustodial parent having alternate weekends and holidays. The presumption only applies when the person labeled the custodial parent has significantly more time with the child. *Cooper v. Kalworf,* 532 S.E. 3d 58, 67 (Ark. 2017).

C. Material change in circumstances test; no factors enumerated for relocation

Georgia. Of the southern states surveyed, Georgia's relocation law appears to be most similar to Mississippi's. Prior to 2003, Georgia law presumed that a custodial parent's move was in the child's best interest. Custody could be modified only if the noncustodial parent proved that the proposed move endangered the child. The Georgia Supreme Court overruled that precedent in *Bodne v. Bodne*, 588 S.E. 2d 728 (Ga. 2003), holding instead that the noncustodial parent has the burden of proving that a custodial parent's relocation is a material change in circumstances and that modification is in the child's best interest. *Id.* at 729. Later interpretations state that a parent's relocation is not automatically a material change in circumstances. Instead, the issue must be decided on a case-by-case basis. Relocation is a factor, but not an automatic reason to modify custody. See *Brazil v. Williams,* 859 S.E. 2d 490 (Ga. Ct. App. 2021).

D. The American Law Institute

The American Law Institute's proposal for relocation attempts to balance the rights of the custodial and noncustodial parent and the child's best interests. See AMERICAN LAW INSTITUTE, PRINCIPLES OF THE LAW OF FAMILY DISSOLUTION, § 2.17(1)(4) (2002) (ALI PRINCIPLES).A move is considered a material change in circumstances if it "significantly impairs either parent's ability to exercise responsibilities the parent has been exercising."

If the relocation makes it impractical to maintain the same schedule of visitation, the court should permit the move if the custodial parent proves that the move is "for a valid purpose, in good faith, and to a location that is reasonable in light of the purpose." Even if a valid purpose is proved, a move is not reasonable if the purpose of the move is "substantially achievable without moving, or by moving to a location that is substantially less disruptive of the other parent's relationship to the child."

If the relocation is approved, the court "should minimize the impairment to a parent-child relationship caused by a parent's relocation through alternative arrangements for the exercise of custodial responsibility."

COLLABORATIVE LAW

By: Mark A. Chinn
Summer School for Lawyers
July 13, 2021

About Mark A. Chinn

Mark Chinn operates Chinn & Associates, a Mississippi statewide practice in family law. He is serving as Chair of the Ad Hoc Committee on Collaborative Law. Mark has been Chair of the Mississippi Bar Family Law Section twice, served on the ABA Family Law Section Council, and currently serves on the ABA Family Law Section Publications Board. He is the author of three ABA books on family law: How to Build and Manage a Family Law Practice, The Constructive Divorce, and Forms, Checklists and Procedures for the Family Lawyer. He has been a frequent speaker for the American Bar Association Family Law Section, The American Academy of Matrimonial Lawyers, State Bar Associations, Mississippi College School of Law, Ole Miss Law School and the Mississippi Bar on issues of family law practice.

I.   Introduction:

Bar President Jennifer Ingram has a keen interest in creating better and more civil avenues for the resolution of civil disputes. At her request, the Board of Bar Commissioners approved a new Ad Hoc Committee ("Committee") for this bar year to study the concept of Collaborative Law, particularly where domestic matters are concerned.

The charge of the Committee is:

> To research the concept of Collaborative Law and study its implementation and effectiveness in states that have adopted The Uniform Collaborative Law Act as an alternative to litigation in domestic relations and other civil litigation matters (i.e. Utah, Nevada, Texas, Hawaii, Ohio, District of Columbia, and Washington State), and to make recommendations to the Commissioners no later than the April 2021 Commissioners meeting as to whether Collaborative Law is a viable, desirable option for Mississippi to implement. In the process of researching the issue, it may be desirable to consult with the Family Law and Alternative Dispute Resolution Sections of the Bar. The ABA also has resources that may be informative on the issue.

Bar President Ingram and I worked together to appoint the following committee members from differing legal backgrounds: Deborah Bell of Oxford, Don Campbell of Jackson, Randy Day of Jackson, Representative Debra Gibbs of Jackson, Reggie Blackledge of Collins, and Susan Steffey of Jackson. Bar President Ingram also attended all of our meetings.

The committee conducted an introductory meeting on September 8, 2020 via zoom. The following questions were developed for exploration:

1. Is there a need to change the law to provide for Collaborative Law? Or can attorneys just sign the agreement without a rule or law change?
2. Is there a role for a mediator in Collaborative Law?
3. Can a judge order Collaborative Law?
4. What are the attorney withdrawal issues?
5. What are the access to justice implications?
6. Can Collaborative Law be used in other practice areas?

With the development of questions, the committee sought input from collaborative law experts from around the country. On October 26, 2020 via Zoom, the committee heard from Jennifer Tull of Austin, TX, Michelle Lawless of Chicago, IL and Adam Cordover of Tampa, FL - all experts in the field.

During this session, it was determined that legislation and/or supreme court rule were essential to getting collaborative law off the ground. The role of the mediator in collaborative law is possible, but not necessary. Judges can order cases to collaborative resolution. The mandatory withdrawal of attorneys from matters that cannot be settled without litigation is the key ingredient to collaborative law. The committee felt that collaborative law could be a great help in access to justice and other legal practice areas.

The committee decided its focus going forward would be attorney education through CLE programs and the like. When appropriate, and with the approval of the Board of Bar Commissioners, the supreme court would be approached for guidance in rule making and possibly legislation.

Our efforts to inform the bar on this subject include scheduling one or more introductory CLE programs on the subject. We have also been given the opportunity to submit the article on the subject for the Mississippi Lawyer, written by Jennifer Tull of Austin, TX, which was published in the Winter 2021 edition of The Mississippi Lawyer.

A report was made to the Board of Bar Commissioners via Zoom, and it was determined that the committee should formulate more specific recommendations on rules and/or legislation. In addition, it was determined that the committee should continue its work in the next bar year with the same chairman and members.

I was invited by the Summer School for Lawyers Program Committee to present on the subject during this summer school session as a part of the process of informing our bar about this new form of alternative dispute resolution.

II.   What is "Collaborative Law" and where did it come from?

Collaborative law is a voluntary, contractually based alternative dispute resolution process for parties who seek to negotiate a resolution of their matter rather than having a ruling imposed upon them by a court or arbitrator. The parties agree that their lawyer's representation is limited to representing them solely for the purposes of negotiation, and that if the matter is not settled, new lawyers will be retained if the matter proceeds to litigation or arbitration. The lawyers and the clients agree to engage in good faith negotiation, share relevant information, the use of joint experts (if experts are needed), client participation in the negotiations, respectful communications, and the confidentiality of the negotiation process.[1]

a. **How did Collaborative Law start?** It is said that Stuart Webb, a family lawyer in Minneapolis, MN, originated the idea in 1990. It spread so rapidly that by the end of a decade, few family law conferences failed to emphasize Collaborative Law as an important new tool for resolving divorce issues. The American Bar Association, The Association of Family and Conciliation Courts, and the American Academy of Matrimonial Lawyers, to name a few, offer workshops and continuing education

---

[1]   Collaborative Law Committee of the ABA Section of Dispute Resolution: Fact Sheet on the Uniform Collaborative Law Rules/Act

presentations to introduce a model to the family law bar.[2]

b. **How has Collaborative Law grown?** One of the biggest agents of growth is the Uniform Law Commission. Uniform laws standardize the most important features of a process. The Uniform Collaborative Law was completed by the Uniform Law Commission in 2009 and amended in 2010. It has been approved by the American Bar Association and has been enacted by 20 states and the District of Columbia. These states include the southern states of Texas, Alabama, Tennessee, North Carolina, and Florida. It is also practiced in every Canadian Providence, Australia, England, France, Germany, and at least 10 other countries.[3]

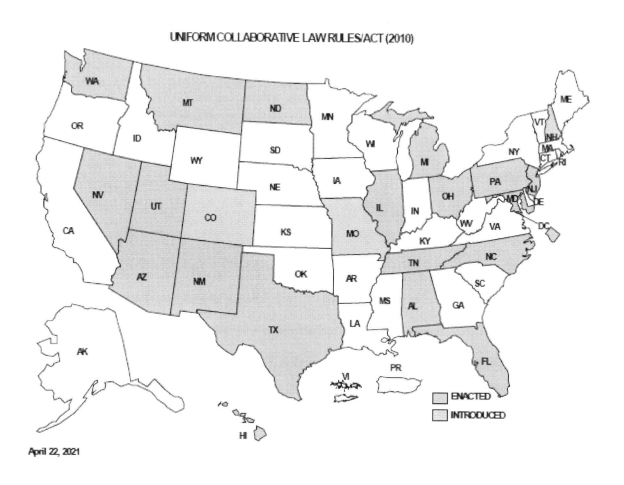

UNIFORM COLLABORATIVE LAW RULES/ACT (2010)

ENACTED

INTRODUCED

April 22, 2021

---

[2] Pauline H. Tesler, Collaborative Law: Achieving Effective Resolution in Divorce Without Litigation xix (2001).

[3] Uniform Law Commission, http://www.uniformlaws.org

c. **What are the essential characteristics of Collaborative Law?** The hallmarks of the process are:

- Full, voluntary, early discovery disclosures.

- Acceptance by the parties of the highest fiduciary duties toward one another, whether imposed by state law or not.

- Voluntary acceptance of a priori of settlement as the goal and respectful, fully participatory process as the means.

- Transparency of process.

- Joint retention of neutral experts.

- Commitment to meeting the legitimate goals of both parties if at all possible.

- Avoidance of even the threat of litigation.

- Disqualification of all lawyers and experts from participation in any legal proceedings between the parties outside the collaborative law process.

- Four-way settlement meetings as the principal means by which negotiations and communications take place.[4]

d. **How is "success" defined?** Lawyers traditionally think of success as being a zealous advocate who is trying to achieve the best results for their client without regard for the impact of result on the other client. In a Collaborative Process, succeeding takes on a new definition: you work toward an outcome that is best not only for your client but for all concerned. Your goal is a workable, durable agreement with which all clients can live. One author has stated that goal is not even "win-win," but a set of decisions that "work-work."[5]

III. **What are the reasons we should do Collaborative Law?**

a. **Divorce is common.** Currently, one of every two marriages in the United States ends in divorce. "Divorce, in other words, is a predictable life passage for marrying couples to anticipate, not a rare catastrophe that happens only to the unlucky or undeserving few."[6]

b. **The typical divorce process is damaging.** "Our litigation system incentivizes the harshest of attacks on the opposing party."[7] Even though all of us litigators know that 95% of cases settle before they go to court, cases often do not settle until after the litigation damage is done to the parties and their children, including massive legal

---

[4] Tesler, *supra* at 8.
[5] Forrest S. Mosten & Adam B. Cordover, Building a Successful Collaborative Family Law Practice 29 (2018).
[6] Tesler, *supra* at 1.
[7] Mosten & Cordover, *supra* at 3.

expenses. Clients who engage in a "demolition approach" to divorce soon realize that once their divorce is completed there is no one to help them put their lives back together.[8]

c. **Litigation hurts lawyers.** Family lawyers occupy a unique position in the legal world. They may be the only group of lawyers that litigate against their competitors. Personal injury lawyers litigate against defense lawyers. Criminal defense lawyers litigate against prosecutors. Family lawyers also represent both husbands and wives, so they litigate against literally everyone. There is no doubt that litigation often creates personal conflict between the lawyers.[9]

d. **Lawyers should be peacemakers.**

Abe Lincoln wrote: "Discourage litigation. Persuade neighbors to compromise whenever you can . . . As a peacemaker, the lawyer has a superior opportunity of becoming a good [person]." [10]

The late Supreme Court Chief Justice Warren Burger made the same point: "The entire legal profession . . . has become so mesmerized with the stimulation of the courtroom contest that we tend to forget that we ought to be healers of conflict."[11]

The Bible commands us to settle with our neighbor on the way to court. Matthew 5:25.

IV. The Key ingredient.

The key ingredient is the commitment of the parties, but more importantly, the lawyers to avoid litigation.[12] Everyone signs an agreement that if there is going to be litigation, the lawyers will not be involved. This puts the responsibility for the outcome of the case on the parties.[13] This means that each lawyer takes on the responsibility for moving each client from artificial bargaining positions to the articulation of real needs and interests.[14] The model simply does not work without the lawyer disqualification provision.[15]

a. **The Lawyer must change his mindset.** Tesler writes on page 16: "Collaborative lawyers have discovered that because resort to the courts means the termination of the collaborative process, their very thinking about dispute resolution changes in important ways compared to how they think when not involved in collaborative law

---

[8] Jennifer Tull, *Collaborative Law: A New Alternative to Family Law Litigation*, The Mississippi Lawyer, Winter 2021 at 12.
[9] Mosten & Cordover, *supra* at xxxii.
[10] *Id.* at 3.
[11] *Id.*
[12] Tesler, *supra* at 6.
[13] Tull, *supra* at 13.
[14] Tesler, *supra* at xxi.
[15] *Id.* at 17.

representation. Litigation for a collaborative lawyer is not merely another item on a menu of dispute-resolution options, as it necessarily must be for even the most collegial of traditional family lawyers. In the collaborative law process, litigation represents a failure of both intention and imagination. Where lawyers think differently, they behave differently and counsel their clients differently." The lawyer must not include "court-based" resolution as a part of the range of solutions.[16]

TABLE 1. Retooling Yourself[16]

Adversarial	Collaborative
The goal is to win	The goal is completing the divorce transition with integrity and mutual satisfaction
"Win Big" is the best outcome	"Win-Win" is the best outcome
Focus on bottom-line outcome limits openness to creative problem-solving	Detachment from outcome permits creative process to occur
Magnitude of immediately quantifiable, measurable outcomes is the benchmark of attorney's success	How well the client's larger life goals are served by the collaborative process is the benchmark of attorney's success
Believes one must be aggressive to win	Understands the difference between aggression and assertion
Views emotions and feelings as distractions from the real work	Views emotions and feelings as important elements of collaborative process that need to be acknowledged and appropriately managed
Hides self	Reveals self
Sees self as gladiator	Sees self as specialist in conflict management and guided negotiations
Believes life experiences happen to us	Believes life experiences are reflections of who we are
Sees forgiveness as weakness	Sees forgiveness as strength
Regards litigation process as template for resolving disputes	Regards litigation as last resort for resolving disputes

b. **"Interest based negotiation."** Tesler writes the following about interest-based negotiation on page 83 of her book: "Interest-based (or needs-based) bargaining is the preferred mode of bargaining employed in collaborative practice. Unlike the bargaining styles commonly used in adversarial legal negotiations, interest-based bargaining requires considerable groundwork between collaborative lawyer and client before any issue is brought to the four-way table for discussion. In this mode of bargaining, lawyer and client examine every one of the client's identified goals and priorities under a microscope, 'peeling the onion' down from what the client initially states as goals and priorities, to examine why the client wants each goal, what benefits achieving the goal

---

[16] Tesler, *supra* at xx.

would bring to the client, whether there might be other ways of achieving the same benefits that are as good or better than the means the client has identified, and whether the goal can be described at the four-way table in terms that any reasonable person of good faith would recognize as legitimate. Since no collaborative agreement will result unless both parties can agree, it follows that presenting goals in the most reasonable manner possible and finding modes of reaching the identified goals that are consistent with the other party's legitimate interests will provide the best chance for win-win settlement – the overriding goal in service of which all collaborative lawyers are retained. Peeling the onion is a kind of work that conventional civil litigators, steeped in the dance of Mediterranean marketplace bargaining, rarely engage in. It is the gateway to lateral thinking, and the key to identifying win-win solutions that expand the settlement pie beyond what is available in court."

TABLE 4. Retooling Negotiations

Adversarial	Collaborative
Assumes litigation paradigm from first meeting with client	Presents the alternate dispute-resolution continuum and offers a variety of options for professional help
Prepares for court battle from very beginning of representation	Considers court as last resort; collaboration first
Strategy is to devise and communicate credible threats	Strategy is to collaborate toward mutually beneficial outcome
Prefers positional bargaining	Prefers interest-based bargaining
Focuses on obstacles in the way of agreement	Challenges reality of obstacles in the way of agreement
Controls process to achieve efficient, task-oriented meetings	Appreciates need for:
	–allowing everyone to be heard and acknowledged
	–creating an environment of honesty and good faith
	–encouraging each party to develop comfort with the other party's lawyer
	–forging process commitments that will be honored
	–incorporating ceremonial elements at start and finish of collaborative process
Sees impasse as gateway to trial	Sees impasse as gateway to enhanced creative process
Resorts to compromise late, as escape from ongoing strains of legal action	Aims always for agreement as first and best resolution of dispute

V. What is the role of Mediation?

a. Collaborative law adopts some of the principles of mediation, but it is regarded as a more powerful and friendly process. Mediation is typically a process that occurs at the end of a discovery process and lasts for a day or so. But, during the mediation, the lawyers and clients often play their traditional adversarial negotiation tactics which often lead to discord, even though the case is settled. Moreover, mediation often contains a pressure component where clients feel they must reach agreement on a given day.[17] In the collaborative process, the lawyers' interest-based negotiation takes place from the very beginning and throughout the process. "Hardball tactics, threats, tactical delays, hidden agendas, and "hide-the-ball" are barred from the process . . ." "If anyone acts in bad faith, uses threats, or resorts to the courts, the process must terminate . . ."[18]

b. Mediators can certainly play a role in the process, as can arbitrators.

VI. Is there a role for collaborative law in delivering service to underserved populations?

Yes, collaborative law can be an excellent tool for assisting legal services and pro bono lawyers in bringing about resolution without conflict or court. For further discussion, see Adam B. Cordover, "Pro Bono Collaborative Divorce: Helping Others While Helping Yourself." Blog post August 26, 2014.

VII. How to get this going.

Here are the elements of creating a successful collaborative law practice in this state and your area:

- **Education.** Lawyers need to educate themselves on this process and buy in to its merit.

- **Identifying like minded people.** Lawyers should identify lawyers in their community who have the same mindset to change the way people resolve their problems: lawyers willing to commit to sign an agreement to disqualify themselves if the process breaks down.

- **Training.** The mindset and process for lawyers is so different from their traditional negotiation approach—which includes the nuclear option (litigation)—that training is essential to success.

- **Start groups.** Lawyers should form collaborative law groups in their communities to support the process.

- **Enabling rules or legislation.** While I do not believe enabling rules or legislation is necessary for collaborative law, as a practical matter, I do not believe it will take root unless the legislature and/or the supreme court put their stamp of approval on rules and/or legislation. The Uniform Act is a good place to start.

---

[17] Tull, *supra* at 16.
[18] Tesler, *supra* at 11.

UNIFORM COLLABORATIVE LAW RULES

and

UNIFORM COLLABORATIVE LAW ACT
(Last Revised or Amended in 2010)

Drafted by the

NATIONAL CONFERENCE OF COMMISSIONERS
ON UNIFORM STATE LAWS

and by it

APPROVED AND RECOMMENDED FOR ENACTMENT
IN ALL THE STATES

at its

ANNUAL CONFERENCE
MEETING IN ITS ONE-HUNDRED-AND-EIGHTEENTH YEAR
IN SANTA FE, NEW MEXICO
JULY 9-16, 2009

WITHOUT PREFATORY NOTE OR COMMENTS

April 24, 2020

Note for enacting states: The provisions for regulation of collaborative law are presented in two formats for enactment- by court rules or legislation. The substantive provisions of each format are identical with the exception of several standard form clauses typically found in legislation. Each state considering adopting the Uniform Collaborative Law Rules (UCLR) or the Uniform Collaborative Law Act (UCLA) should review its practices and precedent to first determine whether the substantive provisions are best adopted by court rule or statute. The decision may vary from state to state depending on the allocation of authority between the legislature and the judiciary for regulation of contracts, alternative dispute resolution, and the legal profession. States may also decide to enact part of the substantive provisions by court rule and part by legislation. Specific comments following some particular rules or sections indicate whether the Drafting Committee recommends enactment by court rule or legislation. Drafting agencies may need to renumber sections and cross references depending on their decision concerning the appropriate method of enactment.

UNIFORM COLLABORATIVE LAW RULES

RULE 1. SHORT TITLE. These rules may be cited as the Uniform Collaborative Law Rules.

RULE 2. DEFINITIONS. In these rules:

(1) "Collaborative law communication" means a statement, whether oral or in a record, or verbal or nonverbal, that:

(A) is made to conduct, participate in, continue, or reconvene a collaborative law process; and

(B) occurs after the parties sign a collaborative law participation agreement and before the collaborative law process is concluded.

(2) "Collaborative law participation agreement" means an agreement by persons to participate in a collaborative law process.

(3) "Collaborative law process" means a procedure intended to resolve a collaborative matter without intervention by a tribunal in which persons:

(A) sign a collaborative law participation agreement; and

(B) are represented by collaborative lawyers.

(4) "Collaborative lawyer" means a lawyer who represents a party in a collaborative law

process.

(5) "Collaborative matter" means a dispute, transaction, claim, problem, or issue for resolution, including a dispute, claim, or issue in a proceeding, which

Alternative A

is described in a collaborative law participation agreement and arises under the family or domestic relations law of this state, including:

(A) marriage, divorce, dissolution, annulment, and property distribution;

(B) child custody, visitation, and parenting time;

(C) alimony, maintenance, and child support;

(D) adoption;

(E) parentage; and

(F) premarital, marital, and post-marital agreements.

Alternative B

is described in a collaborative law participation agreement.

End of Alternatives

(6) "Law firm" means:

(A) lawyers who practice law together in a partnership, professional corporation, sole proprietorship, limited liability company, or association; and

(B) lawyers employed in a legal services organization, or the legal department of a corporation or other organization, or the legal department of a government or governmental subdivision, agency, or instrumentality.

(7) "Nonparty participant" means a person, other than a party and the party's collaborative lawyer, that participates in a collaborative law process.

(8) "Party" means a person that signs a collaborative law participation agreement and

whose consent is necessary to resolve a collaborative matter.

(9) "Person" means an individual, corporation, business trust, estate, trust, partnership, limited liability company, association, joint venture, public corporation, government or governmental subdivision, agency, or instrumentality, or any other legal or commercial entity.

(10) "Proceeding" means:

(A) a judicial, administrative, arbitral, or other adjudicative process before a tribunal, including related prehearing and post-hearing motions, conferences, and discovery; or

(B) a legislative hearing or similar process.

(11) "Prospective party" means a person that discusses with a prospective collaborative lawyer the possibility of signing a collaborative law participation agreement.

(12) "Record" means information that is inscribed on a tangible medium or that is stored in an electronic or other medium and is retrievable in perceivable form.

(13) "Related to a collaborative matter" means involving the same parties, transaction or occurrence, nucleus of operative fact, dispute, claim, or issue as the collaborative matter.

(14) "Sign" means, with present intent to authenticate or adopt a record:

(A) to execute or adopt a tangible symbol; or

(B) to attach to or logically associate with the record an electronic symbol, sound, or process.

(15) "Tribunal" means:

(A) a court, arbitrator, administrative agency, or other body acting in an adjudicative capacity which, after presentation of evidence or legal argument, has jurisdiction to render a decision affecting a party's interests in a matter; or

(B) a legislative body conducting a hearing or similar process.

RULE 3. APPLICABILITY. These rules apply to a collaborative law participation agreement that meets the requirements of Rule 4 signed [on or] after [the effective date of the rules].

RULE 4. COLLABORATIVE LAW PARTICIPATION AGREEMENT; REQUIREMENTS.

(a) A collaborative law participation agreement must:

(1) be in a record;

(2) be signed by the parties;

(3) state the parties' intention to resolve a collaborative matter through a collaborative law process under these rules;

(4) describe the nature and scope of the matter;

(5) identify the collaborative lawyer who represents each party in the process; and

(6) contain a statement by each collaborative lawyer confirming the lawyer's representation of a party in the collaborative law process.

(b) Parties may agree to include in a collaborative law participation agreement additional provisions not inconsistent with these rules.

RULE 5. BEGINNING AND CONCLUDING COLLABORATIVE LAW PROCESS.

(a) A collaborative law process begins when the parties sign a collaborative law participation agreement.

(b) A tribunal may not order a party to participate in a collaborative law process over that party's objection.

(c) A collaborative law process is concluded by a:

(1) resolution of a collaborative matter as evidenced by a signed record;

(2) resolution of a part of the collaborative matter, evidenced by a signed record, in which the parties agree that the remaining parts of the matter will not be resolved in the process; or

(3) termination of the process.

(d) A collaborative law process terminates:

(1) when a party gives notice to other parties in a record that the process is ended;

(2) when a party:

(A) begins a proceeding related to a collaborative matter without the agreement of all parties; or

(B) in a pending proceeding related to the matter:

(i) initiates a pleading, motion, order to show cause, or request for a conference with the tribunal;

(ii) requests that the proceeding be put on the [tribunal's active calendar]; or

(iii) takes similar action requiring notice to be sent to the parties; or

(3) except as otherwise provided by subsection (g), when a party discharges a collaborative lawyer or a collaborative lawyer withdraws from further representation of a party.

(e) A party's collaborative lawyer shall give prompt notice to all other parties in a record of a discharge or withdrawal.

(f) A party may terminate a collaborative law process with or without cause.

(g) Notwithstanding the discharge or withdrawal of a collaborative lawyer, a collaborative law process continues, if not later than 30 days after the date that the notice of the discharge or withdrawal of a collaborative lawyer required by subsection (e) is sent to the parties:

(1) the unrepresented party engages a successor collaborative lawyer; and

(2) in a signed record:

(A) the parties consent to continue the process by reaffirming the collaborative law participation agreement;

(B) the agreement is amended to identify the successor collaborative lawyer; and

(C) the successor collaborative lawyer confirms the lawyer's representation of a party in the collaborative process.

(h) A collaborative law process does not conclude if, with the consent of the parties, a party requests a tribunal to approve a resolution of the collaborative matter or any part thereof as evidenced by a signed record.

(i) A collaborative law participation agreement may provide additional methods of concluding a collaborative law process.

RULE 6. PROCEEDINGS PENDING BEFORE TRIBUNAL; STATUS REPORT.

(a) Persons in a proceeding pending before a tribunal may sign a collaborative law participation agreement to seek to resolve a collaborative matter related to the proceeding. The parties shall file promptly with the tribunal a notice of the agreement after it is signed. Subject to subsection (c) and Rules 7 and 8, the filing operates as an application for a stay of the proceeding.

(b) The parties shall file promptly with the tribunal notice in a record when a collaborative law process concludes. The stay of the proceeding under subsection (a) is lifted when the notice is filed. The notice may not specify any reason for termination of the process.

(c) A tribunal in which a proceeding is stayed under subsection (a) may require the parties and collaborative lawyers to provide a status report on the collaborative law process and the proceeding. A status report may include only information on whether the process is ongoing

or concluded. It may not include a report, assessment, evaluation, recommendation, finding, or

other communication regarding a collaborative law process or collaborative law matter.

(d) A tribunal may not consider a communication made in violation of subsection (c).

(e) A tribunal shall provide parties notice and an opportunity to be heard before

dismissing a proceeding in which a notice of collaborative process is filed based on delay or

failure to prosecute.

Legislative Note: In enacting this Rule, states should review existing provisions concerning stays of pending proceedings when the parties agree to engage in alternative dispute resolution. As noted in the comment to Rule 6, some states treat party entry into an alternative dispute resolution procedure such as collaborative law or mediation as an application for a stay, which the court has discretion to grant or deny, while other states make the stay mandatory. Enacting states may wish to duplicate the practice currently applicable to collaborative law, mediation, or other forms of alternative dispute resolution.

RULE 7. EMERGENCY ORDER. During a collaborative law process, a tribunal may

issue emergency orders to protect the health, safety, welfare, or interest of a party or [insert term

for family or household member as defined in [state civil protection order statute]].

RULE 8. APPROVAL OF AGREEMENT BY TRIBUNAL. A tribunal may approve

an agreement resulting from a collaborative law process.

RULE 9. DISQUALIFICATION OF COLLABORATIVE LAWYER AND

LAWYERS IN ASSOCIATED LAW FIRM.

(a) Except as otherwise provided in subsection (c), a collaborative lawyer is disqualified

from appearing before a tribunal to represent a party in a proceeding related to the collaborative

matter.

(b) Except as otherwise provided in subsection (c) and Rules 10 and 11, a lawyer in a law

firm with which the collaborative lawyer is associated is disqualified from appearing before a

tribunal to represent a party in a proceeding related to the collaborative matter if the collaborative lawyer is disqualified from doing so under subsection (a).

(c) A collaborative lawyer or a lawyer in a law firm with which the collaborative lawyer is associated may represent a party:

(1) to ask a tribunal to approve an agreement resulting from the collaborative law process; or

(2) to seek or defend an emergency order to protect the health, safety, welfare, or interest of a party, or [insert term for family or household member as defined in [state civil protection order statute]] if a successor lawyer is not immediately available to represent that person.

(d) If subsection (c)(2) applies, a collaborative lawyer, or lawyer in a law firm with which the collaborative lawyer is associated, may represent a party or [insert term for family or household member] only until the person is represented by a successor lawyer or reasonable measures are taken to protect the health, safety, welfare, or interest of the person.

RULE 10. LOW INCOME PARTIES.

(a) The disqualification of Rule 9(a) applies to a collaborative lawyer representing a party with or without fee.

(b) After a collaborative law process concludes, another lawyer in a law firm with which a collaborative lawyer disqualified under Rule 9(a) is associated may represent a party without fee in the collaborative matter or a matter related to the collaborative matter if:

(1) the party has an annual income that qualifies the party for free legal representation under the criteria established by the law firm for free legal representation;

(2) the collaborative law participation agreement so provides; and

(3) the collaborative lawyer is isolated from any participation in the collaborative matter or a matter related to the collaborative matter through procedures within the law firm

which are reasonably calculated to isolate the collaborative lawyer from such participation.

RULE 11. GOVERNMENTAL ENTITY AS PARTY.

(a) The disqualification of Rule 9(a) applies to a collaborative lawyer representing a party that is a government or governmental subdivision, agency, or instrumentality.

(b) After a collaborative law process concludes, another lawyer in a law firm with which the collaborative lawyer is associated may represent a government or governmental subdivision, agency, or instrumentality in the collaborative matter or a matter related to the collaborative matter if:

(1) the collaborative law participation agreement so provides; and

(2) the collaborative lawyer is isolated from any participation in the collaborative matter or a matter related to the collaborative matter through procedures within the law firm which are reasonably calculated to isolate the collaborative lawyer from such participation.

RULE 12. DISCLOSURE OF INFORMATION.

Except as provided by law other than these rules, during the collaborative law process, on the request of another party, a party shall make timely, full, candid, and informal disclosure of information related to the collaborative matter without formal discovery. A party also shall update promptly previously disclosed information that has materially changed. The parties may define the scope of disclosure during the collaborative law process.

RULE 13. STANDARDS OF PROFESSIONAL RESPONSIBILITY AND MANDATORY REPORTING NOT AFFECTED.

These rules do not affect:

(1) the professional responsibility obligations and standards applicable to a lawyer or other licensed professional; or

(2) the obligation of a person to report abuse or neglect, abandonment, or exploitation of a child or adult under the law of this state.

RULE 14. APPROPRIATENESS OF COLLABORATIVE LAW PROCESS.

Before a prospective party signs a collaborative law participation agreement, a prospective collaborative lawyer shall:

(1) assess with the prospective party factors the lawyer reasonably believes relate to whether a collaborative law process is appropriate for the prospective party's matter;

(2) provide the prospective party with information that the lawyer reasonably believes is sufficient for the party to make an informed decision about the material benefits and risks of a collaborative law process as compared to the material benefits and risks of other reasonably available alternatives for resolving the proposed collaborative matter, such as litigation, mediation, arbitration, or expert evaluation; and

(3) advise the prospective party that:

(A) after signing an agreement if a party initiates a proceeding or seeks tribunal intervention in a pending proceeding related to the collaborative matter, the collaborative law process terminates;

(B) participation in a collaborative law process is voluntary and any party has the right to terminate unilaterally a collaborative law process with or without cause; and

(C) the collaborative lawyer and any lawyer in a law firm with which the collaborative lawyer is associated may not appear before a tribunal to represent a party in a proceeding related to the collaborative matter, except as authorized by Rule 9(c), 10(b), or 11(b).

RULE 15. COERCIVE OR VIOLENT RELATIONSHIP.

(a) Before a prospective party signs a collaborative law participation agreement, a prospective collaborative lawyer shall make reasonable inquiry whether the prospective party has a history of a coercive or violent relationship with another prospective party.

(b) Throughout a collaborative law process, a collaborative lawyer reasonably and continuously shall assess whether the party the collaborative lawyer represents has a history of a coercive or violent relationship with another party.

(c) If a collaborative lawyer reasonably believes that the party the lawyer represents or the prospective party who consults the lawyer has a history of a coercive or violent relationship with another party or prospective party, the lawyer may not begin or continue a collaborative law process unless:

(1) the party or the prospective party requests beginning or continuing a process; and

(2) the collaborative lawyer reasonably believes that the safety of the party or prospective party can be protected adequately during a process.

RULE 16. CONFIDENTIALITY OF COLLABORATIVE LAW COMMUNICATION.

A collaborative law communication is confidential to the extent agreed by the parties in a signed record or as provided by law of this state other than these rules.

RULE 17. PRIVILEGE AGAINST DISCLOSURE FOR COLLABORATIVE LAW COMMUNICATION; ADMISSIBILITY; DISCOVERY.

(a) Subject to Rules 18 and 19, a collaborative law communication is privileged under subsection (b), is not subject to discovery, and is not admissible in evidence.

(b) In a proceeding, the following privileges apply:

(1) A party may refuse to disclose, and may prevent any other person from disclosing, a collaborative law communication.

(2) A nonparty participant may refuse to disclose, and may prevent any other person from disclosing, a collaborative law communication of the nonparty participant.

(c) Evidence or information that is otherwise admissible or subject to discovery does not become inadmissible or protected from discovery solely because of its disclosure or use in a collaborative law process.

RULE 18. WAIVER AND PRECLUSION OF PRIVILEGE.

(a) A privilege under Rule 17 may be waived in a record or orally during a proceeding if it is expressly waived by all parties and, in the case of the privilege of a nonparty participant, it is also expressly waived by the nonparty participant.

(b) A person that makes a disclosure or representation about a collaborative law communication which prejudices another person in a proceeding may not assert a privilege under Rule 17, but this preclusion applies only to the extent necessary for the person prejudiced to respond to the disclosure or representation.

RULE 19. LIMITS OF PRIVILEGE.

(a) There is no privilege under Rule 17 for a collaborative law communication that is:

(1) available to the public under [state open records act] or made during a session of a collaborative law process that is open, or is required by law to be open, to the public;

(2) a threat or statement of a plan to inflict bodily injury or commit a crime of violence;

(3) intentionally used to plan a crime, commit or attempt to commit a crime, or conceal an ongoing crime or ongoing criminal activity; or

(4) in an agreement resulting from the collaborative law process, evidenced by a record signed by all parties to the agreement.

(b) The privileges under Rule 17 for a collaborative law communication do not apply to the extent that a communication is:

(1) sought or offered to prove or disprove a claim or complaint of professional misconduct or malpractice arising from or related to a collaborative law process; or

(2) sought or offered to prove or disprove abuse, neglect, abandonment, or

exploitation of a child or adult, unless the [child protective services agency or adult protective services agency] is a party to or otherwise participates in the process.

(c) There is no privilege under Rule 17 if a tribunal finds, after a hearing in camera, that the party seeking discovery or the proponent of the evidence has shown the evidence is not otherwise available, the need for the evidence substantially outweighs the interest in protecting confidentiality, and the collaborative law communication is sought or offered in:

(1) a court proceeding involving a felony [or misdemeanor]; or

(2) a proceeding seeking rescission or reformation of a contract arising out of the collaborative law process or in which a defense to avoid liability on the contract is asserted.

(d) If a collaborative law communication is subject to an exception under subsection (b) or (c), only the part of the communication necessary for the application of the exception may be disclosed or admitted.

(e) Disclosure or admission of evidence excepted from the privilege under subsection (b) or (c) does not make the evidence or any other collaborative law communication discoverable or admissible for any other purpose.

(f) The privileges under Rule 17 do not apply if the parties agree in advance in a signed record, or if a record of a proceeding reflects agreement by the parties, that all or part of a collaborative law process is not privileged. This subsection does not apply to a collaborative law communication made by a person that did not receive actual notice of the agreement before the communication was made.

RULE 20. AUTHORITY OF TRIBUNAL IN CASE OF NONCOMPLIANCE.

(a) If an agreement fails to meet the requirements of Rule 4, or a lawyer fails to comply with Rule 14 or 15, a tribunal may nonetheless find that the parties intended to enter into a collaborative law participation agreement if they:

(1) signed a record indicating an intention to enter into a collaborative law participation agreement; and

(2) reasonably believed they were participating in a collaborative law process.

(b) If a tribunal makes the findings specified in subsection (a), and the interests of justice require, the tribunal may:

(1) enforce an agreement evidenced by a record resulting from the process in which the parties participated;

(2) apply the disqualification provisions of Rules 5, 6, 9, 10, and 11; and

(3) apply a privilege under Rule 17.

RULE 21. EFFECTIVE DATE. These rules take effect............

MISSISSIPPI COLLABORATIVE LAW RULE

as proposed by the Mississippi Bar Collaborative Law Study Committee

Rule 1: Short Title. This Rule may be cited as the Uniform Collaborative Law Rule.

Rule 2: Definitions. In this Rule:

1) "Collaborative law communication" means a statement, whether oral or in a record, or verbal or nonverbal, that:

   A. is made to conduct, participate in, continue, or reconvene a collaborative law process; and

   B. occurs after the parties sign a collaborative law participation agreement and before the collaborative law process is concluded.

2) "Collaborative law participation agreement" means an agreement by persons to participate in a collaborative law process.

3) "Collaborative law process" means a procedure intended to resolve a collaborative matter without intervention by a tribunal in which persons:

   A. sign a collaborative law participation agreement; and

   B. are represented by collaborative lawyers.

4) "Collaborative lawyer" means a lawyer who represents a party in a collaborative law process.

5) "Collaborative matter" means a dispute, transaction, claim, problem, or issue for resolution, including a dispute, claim, or issue in a proceeding, which is described in a collaborative law participation agreement and arises under the family or domestic relations law of this state, including:

   A. marriage, divorce, dissolution, annulment, and property distribution;

   B. child custody, visitation, and parenting time;

   C. alimony, maintenance, and child support;

   D. adoption;

   E. parentage;

   F. premarital, marital, and post-marital agreements; and

   G. post Order actions such as modifications, enforcements and contempts.

6) "Law firm" means:

   A. lawyers who practice law together in a partnership, professional corporation, sole proprietorship, limited liability company, or association; and

   B. lawyers employed in a legal services organization, or the legal department of a corporation or other organization, or the legal department of a government or governmental subdivision, agency, or instrumentality.

7) "Nonparty participant" means a person, other than a party and the party's collaborative lawyer, that participates in a collaborative law process.

8) "Party" means a person that signs a collaborative law participation agreement and whose consent is necessary to resolve a collaborative matter.

9) "Prospective party" means a person that discusses with a prospective collaborative lawyer the possibility of signing a collaborative law participation agreement.

10) "Record" means information that is inscribed on a tangible medium or that is stored in an electronic or other medium and is retrievable in perceivable form.

11) "Related to a collaborative matter" means involving the same parties, transaction or occurrence, nucleus of operative fact, dispute, claim, or issue as the collaborative matter.

Rule 3: Applicability. ["Omitted."]

Rule 4: Collaborative Law Participation Agreement; Requirements.

a. A collaborative law participation agreement must:

    1. be in a record;

    2. be signed by the parties;

    3. state the parties' intention to resolve a collaborative matter through a collaborative law process under this Rule;

    4. describe the nature and scope of the matter;

    5. identify the collaborative lawyer who represents each party in the process;

    6. contain a statement by each collaborative lawyer confirming the lawyer's representation of a party in the collaborative law process; and

    7. contain a statement that the parties will forego court intervention while using the collaborative family law process; a statement that they will jointly engage any professionals, experts, etc. in a neutral capacity; and a statement about mandatory disqualification of the collaborative lawyer.

b. Parties may agree to include in a collaborative law participation agreement additional provisions not inconsistent with this Rule.

c. Participation of Collaborative Law attorneys is limited in scope as permitted by Rule 1.2(c) of the Mississippi Rules of Professional Conduct.

Rule 5: Beginning and Concluding Collaborative Law Process.

a. A collaborative law process begins when the parties sign a collaborative law participation agreement.

b. Collaborative law is voluntary and a tribunal may not order a party to participate in a collaborative law process over that party's objection.

c. A collaborative law process is concluded by a:

    1. resolution of a collaborative matter as evidenced by a signed record;

    2. resolution of a part of the collaborative matter, evidenced by a signed record, in which the parties agree that the remaining parts of the matter will not be resolved in the process; or

    3. termination of the process.

d. A collaborative law process terminates:

1. when a party gives notice to other parties in a record that the process is ended;

2. when a party:

    A. begins a proceeding related to a collaborative matter without the agreement of all parties; or

    B. in a pending proceeding related to the matter:

    > i.   initiates a pleading, motion, order to show cause, or request for a conference with the tribunal;
    >
    > ii. requests that the proceeding be put on the [tribunal's active calendar]; or
    >
    > iii. takes similar action requiring notice to be sent to the parties; or

3. except as otherwise provided by subsection (g), when a party discharges a collaborative lawyer or a collaborative lawyer withdraws from further representation of a party.

e. A party's collaborative lawyer shall give prompt notice to all other parties in a record of a discharge or withdrawal.

f. A party may terminate a collaborative law process with or without cause.

g. Notwithstanding the discharge or withdrawal of a collaborative lawyer, a collaborative law process continues, if not later than 30 days after the date that the notice of the discharge or withdrawal of a collaborative lawyer required by subsection (e) is sent to the parties:

1. the unrepresented party engages a successor collaborative lawyer; and

2. in a signed record:

    A. the parties consent to continue the process by reaffirming the collaborative law participation agreement;

    B. the agreement is amended to identify the successor collaborative lawyer; and

    C. the successor collaborative lawyer confirms the lawyer's representation of a party in the collaborative process.

h. A collaborative law process does not conclude if, with the consent of the parties, a party requests a tribunal to approve a resolution of the collaborative matter or any part thereof as evidenced by a signed record.

i. A collaborative law participation agreement may provide additional methods of concluding a collaborative law process.

Rule 6: Proceedings Pending Before Tribunal; Status Report. ["Omitted"]

Rule 7: Emergency Order. During a collaborative law process, a tribunal may issue emergency orders to protect the health, safety, welfare, or interest of a party or other individuals related by consanguinity or affinity who reside with a party or who formerly resided with a party if the emergency order is granted without the agreement of all parties, the granting of the order terminates the collaborative process.

Rule 8: Approval of Agreement by Tribunal. A tribunal may approve an agreement resulting from a collaborative law process.

Rule 9: Disqualification of Collaborative Lawyer and Lawyers in Associated Law Firm.

a. Except as otherwise provided in subsection (c), a collaborative lawyer is disqualified from appearing before a tribunal to represent a party in a proceeding related to the collaborative matter.

b. Except as otherwise provided in subsection (c), a lawyer in a law firm with which the collaborative lawyer is associated is disqualified from appearing before a tribunal to represent a party in a proceeding related to the collaborative matter if the collaborative lawyer is disqualified from doing so under subsection (a).

c. A collaborative lawyer or a lawyer in a law firm with which the collaborative lawyer is associated may represent a party:

   1. to ask a tribunal to approve an agreement resulting from the collaborative law process; or

   2. to seek or defend an emergency order to protect the health, safety, welfare, or interest of a party, or other individuals related by consanguinity or affinity who reside with a party or who formerly resided with a party if a successor lawyer is not immediately available to represent that person.

d. If subsection (c)(2) applies, a collaborative lawyer, or lawyer in a law firm with which the collaborative lawyer is associated, may represent a party or other individuals related by consanguinity or affinity who reside with a party or who formerly resided with a party only until the person is represented by a successor lawyer or reasonable measures are taken to protect the health, safety, welfare, or interest of the person.

Rule 10: Low Income Parties. ["Omitted."].

Rule 11: Governmental Entity as Party. ["Omitted."].

Rule 12: Disclosure of Information.
Except as provided by law other than this Rule, during the collaborative law process, on the request of another party, a party shall make timely, full, candid, and informal disclosure of information related to the collaborative matter without formal discovery. A party also shall update promptly previously disclosed information that has materially changed. The parties may define the scope of disclosure during the collaborative law process.

Rule 13: Standards of Professional Responsibility and Mandatory Reporting Not Affected.
This Rule does not affect:

   1. the professional responsibility obligations and standards applicable to a lawyer or other licensed professional; or

   2. the obligation of a person to report abuse or neglect, abandonment, or exploitation of a child or adult under the law of this state.

Rule 14: Appropriateness of Collaborative Law Process.
Before a prospective party signs a collaborative law participation agreement, a prospective collaborative lawyer shall:

   1. assess with the prospective party factors the lawyer reasonably believes relate to whether a collaborative law process is appropriate for the prospective party's matter;

2.   provide the prospective party with information that the lawyer reasonably believes is sufficient for the party to make an informed decision about the material benefits and risks of a collaborative law process as compared to the material benefits and risks of other reasonably available alternatives for resolving the proposed collaborative matter, such as litigation, mediation, arbitration, or expert evaluation; and

3.   advise the prospective party that:

A.   after signing an agreement if a party initiates a proceeding or seeks tribunal intervention in a pending proceeding related to the collaborative matter, the collaborative law process terminates;

B.   participation in a collaborative law process is voluntary and any party has the right to terminate unilaterally a collaborative law process with or without cause; and

C.   the collaborative lawyer and any lawyer in a law firm with which the collaborative lawyer is associated may not appear before a tribunal to represent a party in a proceeding related to the collaborative matter, except as authorized by Rule 9(c).

Rule 15: Coercive or Violent Relationship. A collaborative lawyer should be aware of the dynamics of domestic violence and take into consideration, in assessing whether to begin or continue a collaborative process, whether the parties have a history of a coercive or violent relationship and whether the safety of the parties can be protected adequately during a collaborative process.

Rule 16: Confidentiality of Collaborative Law Communication. A collaborative law communication is confidential to the extent agreed by the parties in a signed record or as provided by law of this state other than this Rule.

Rule 17: Privilege Against Disclosure for Collaborative Law Communication; Admissibility; Discovery.

a.   Subject to Rules 18 and 19, a collaborative law communication is privileged under subsection (b), is not subject to discovery, and is not admissible in evidence.

b.   In a proceeding, the following privileges apply:

1.   A party may refuse to disclose, and may prevent any other person from disclosing, a collaborative law communication.

2.   A nonparty participant may refuse to disclose, and may prevent any other person from disclosing, a collaborative law communication of the nonparty participant.

c.   Evidence or information that is otherwise admissible or subject to discovery does not become inadmissible or protected from discovery solely because of its disclosure or use in a collaborative law process.

Rule 18: Waiver and Preclusion of Privilege.

a.   A privilege under Rule 17 may be waived in a record or orally during a proceeding if it is expressly waived by all parties and, in the case of the privilege of a nonparty participant, it is also expressly waived by the nonparty participant.

b.   A person that makes a disclosure or representation about a collaborative law communication which prejudices another person in a proceeding may not assert a privilege under

Rule 17, but this preclusion applies only to the extent necessary for the person prejudiced to respond to the disclosure or representation.

Rule 19: Limits of Privilege.

a.   There is no privilege under Rule 17 for a collaborative law communication that is:

    1.   available to the public under the state open records act or made during a session of a collaborative law process that is open, or is required by law to be open, to the public;

    2.   a threat or statement of a plan to inflict bodily injury or commit a crime of violence;

    3.   intentionally used to plan a crime, commit or attempt to commit a crime, or conceal an ongoing crime or ongoing criminal activity; or

    4.   in an agreement resulting from the collaborative law process, evidenced by a record signed by all parties.

b.   The privileges under Rule 17 for a collaborative law communication do not apply to the extent that a communication is:

    1.   sought or offered to prove or disprove a claim or complaint of professional misconduct or malpractice arising from or related to a collaborative law process; or

    2.   sought or offered to prove or disprove abuse, neglect, abandonment, or exploitation of a child or adult, unless the child protective services agency or adult protective services agency is a party to or otherwise participates in the process.

c.   There is no privilege under Rule 17 if a tribunal finds, after a hearing in camera, that the party seeking discovery or the proponent of the evidence has shown the evidence is not otherwise available, the need for the evidence substantially outweighs the interest in protecting confidentiality, and the collaborative law communication is sought or offered in:

    1.   a court proceeding involving a felony or misdemeanor; or

    2.   a proceeding seeking rescission or reformation of a contract arising out of the collaborative law process or in which a defense to avoid liability on the contract is asserted.

d.   If a collaborative law communication is subject to an exception under subsection (b) or (c), only the part of the communication necessary for the application of the exception may be disclosed or admitted.

e.   Disclosure or admission of evidence excepted from the privilege under subsection (b) or (c) does not make the evidence or any other collaborative law communication discoverable or admissible for any other purpose.

f.   The privileges under Rule 17 do not apply if the parties agree in advance in a signed record, or if a record of a proceeding reflects agreement by the parties, that all or part of a collaborative law process is not privileged. This subsection does not apply to a collaborative law communication made by a person that did not receive actual notice of the agreement before the communication was made.

Rule 20: Authority of Tribunal in Case of Noncompliance.

a. If an agreement fails to meet the requirements of Rule 4, or a lawyer fails to comply with Rule 14 or 15, a tribunal may nonetheless find that the parties intended to enter into a collaborative law participation agreement if they:

    1. signed a record indicating an intention to enter into a collaborative law participation agreement; and

    2. reasonably believed they were participating in a collaborative law process.

b. If a tribunal makes the findings specified in subsection (a), and the interests of justice require, the tribunal may:

    1. enforce an agreement evidenced by a record resulting from the process in which the parties participated;

    2. apply the disqualification provisions of Rules 5 and 9; and apply a privilege under Rule 17.

Rule 21: Uniformity of Application and Construction. In applying and construing this uniform rule, consideration must be given to the need to promote uniformity of the law with respect to its subject matter among states that enact it.

Rule 22: Relation to Electronic Signatures in Global and National Commerce Act. This Rule modifies, limits, and supersedes the federal Electronic Signatures in Global and National Commerce Act, 15 U.S.C. Section 7001, et seq., but does not modify, limit, or supersede Section 101(c) of that act, 15 U.S.C Section 7001(c), or authorize electronic delivery of any of the notices described in Section 103(b) of that act, 15 U.S.C. Section 7003(b).

Rule 23: Severability. If any provision of this Rule or its application to any person or circumstance is held invalid, the invalidity does not affect other provisions or applications of this Rule which can be given effect without the invalid provision or application, and to this end the provisions of this Rule are severable.

Rule 24: Effective Date. This Rule takes effect _____.

ETHICS ISSUES IN COLLABORATIVE LAW

I.   THE RULES OF PROFESSIONAL RESPONSIBILITY ARE NOT AFFECTED BY THE PROPOSED RULES.

Proposed Collaborative Law Rule 13 (Standards of Professional Responsibility and Mandatory Reporting Not Affected) provides: "This Rule does not affect: (1) the professional responsibility obligations and standards applicable to a lawyer or other licensed professional; or (2) the obligation of a person to report abuse or neglect, abandonment, or exploitation of a child or adult under the law of this state."

To the extent the proposed rules address ethics issues, they describe what collaborative law attorneys should do to meet the requirements of the Mississippi Rules of Professional Responsibility. The discussion below highlights some of the most commonly raised questions about application of professional responsibility rules to collaborative practice.

II.   DOES THE WITHDRAWAL REQUIREMENT VIOLATE RULES OF PROFESSIONAL RESPONSIBILITY?

The withdrawal requirement is a key element of collaborative practice. All parties and attorneys agree that if the case proceeds to litigation, the parties' attorneys must withdraw. Furthermore, their firm is disqualified from representing the client in litigation in the matter. The American Bar Association and at least six state bar ethics committees have concluded that the withdrawal requirement is consistent with rules of professional responsibility, so long as the client has given informed consent and the limitation is reasonable under the circumstances. See Formal Opinion 07-447, Ethical Considerations in Collaborative Law Practice, ABA Standing Committee on Ethics and Professional Responsibility, August 9, 2007.

MISS. R. PROF. RESP Rule 1.2(c) provides, "A lawyer may limit the objectives or scope of the representation if the limitation is reasonable under the circumstances and the client gives informed consent." The comments state that "the terms upon which representation is undertaken may exclude specific means that might otherwise be used to accomplish the client's objectives." MISS. R. PROF. RESP Rule 1.2(c), Comment.

Proposed Collaborative Practice Rule 14 (Appropriateness of Collaborative Law Process) addresses the need for informed consent, specifically requiring that the lawyer inform the client of the lawyer's limited responsibility under the collaborative law agreement. Proposed Rule 14 also states that the limitation must be reasonable under the circumstances. The presence of domestic violence is a circumstance that may make collaborative divorce unreasonable.

Proposed Collaborative Practice Rule 15 (Coercive or Violent Relationship) states, "A collaborative lawyer should be aware of the dynamics of domestic violence and take into consideration, in assessing whether to begin or continue a collaborative process, whether the parties have a history of a coercive or violent relationship and whether the safety of the parties can be protected adequately during a collaborative process." It would also make sense that a collaborative process would not be reasonable if the lawyer believes that the parties are unlikely to reach a resolution outside of court.

III. How does the collaborative lawyer comply with informed consent requirements?

MISS. R. PROF. RESP. 1.4(b) provides "A lawyer shall explain a matter to the extent reasonably necessary to permit the client to make informed decisions regarding the representation."

MISS. R. PROF. RESP. 1.2(a) provides "A lawyer shall abide by a client's decisions concerning the objectives of representation, . . . and shall consult with the client as to the means by which they are to be pursued. A lawyer shall abide by a client's decision whether to accept an offer of settlement of a matter.

Attorneys who offer collaborative law as an option should be careful to explain the key features of the process to ensure compliance with these rules. Proposed Collaborative Law Rule 14 expands on the lawyer's obligation to inform a client considering collaborative divorce. The Rule requires that the lawyer assess the appropriateness of collaborative practice for the case and provide the client with enough information to make an informed decision about collaborative practice as compared to mediation or litigation. The rule also specifically requires that the lawyer inform the client that (1) the process terminates upon the filing of litigation and that the lawyer must withdraw; (2) the process is voluntary and may be terminated at any time; and (3) upon termination, neither the lawyer nor anyone in the lawyer's firm may represent the client in litigation of the matter.

IV. Does the process unreasonably hinder the lawyer's duty of diligence?

MISS. R. PROF. RESP. 1.4 states that lawyers must act with "reasonable diligence" on behalf of a client. The comments state that "A lawyer should act with commitment and dedication to the interests of the client and with zeal in advocacy upon the client's behalf. However, a lawyer is not bound to press for every advantage that might be realized for a client."

Collaborative practice is based on an agreement to work openly and cooperatively with the opposing party and attorney – to share relevant documents and financial information, to consider the interests of both parents, and to seek experts who are engaged to assist both parties. This approach undoubtedly requires that attorneys not pursue some tactics that would be appropriate in litigation. If the client has agreed to this approach based on informed consent, the lawyer's collaborative approach should satisfy the duty of diligence by meeting the goals of a client who has chosen the collaborative process.

V. Does the agreement to share information violate the lawyer's duty of confidentiality?

MISS. R. PROF. RESP. provides, "A lawyer shall not reveal information relating to the representation of a client unless the client gives informed consent [or] the disclosure is impliedly authorized in order to carry out the representation."

In the collaborative process, attorneys and parties are *required* to share information with the opposing party and attorney. It is critical that attorneys advise clients considering collaborative law the type of information that must be disclosed voluntarily and explain how that process differs from traditional representation. The attorney must secure the client's informed consent to the voluntary disclosure – if the client has concerns about that aspect of the practice, collaborative divorce should not be pursued.

If the client withholds information during the process, the attorney will still be bound by the confidentiality rules of the rules of professional responsibility, which will override the agreement. However, the agreement will usually provide for the attorneys' withdrawal under those circumstances.

VI. DOES THE ATTORNEY'S AGREEMENT WITH THE OPPOSING PARTY CREATE A CONFLICT OF INTERESTS?

MISS. R. PROF. RESP. 1.7(b) provides: A lawyer shall not represent a client if the representation of that client may be materially limited by the lawyer's responsibilities to another client or to a third person, or by the lawyer's own interests, unless the lawyer reasonably believes: (1) the representation will not be adversely affected; and (2) the client has given knowing and informed consent after consultation. The consultation shall include explanation of the implications of the representation and the advantages and risks involved.

The Colorado Ethics Board in 2005 issued an opinion that collaborative practice created a conflict of interest. The opinion stated that the practice "violates Rule 1.7(b) of Colorado Rules of Professional Conduct insofar as a lawyer participating in the process enters into a contractual agreement with the opposing party requiring the lawyer to withdraw in the event that the process is unsuccessful." The Ethics Committee concluded that a client could not consent because of the significant risk that a conflict will materialize. Colo. Bar Ass'n Ethics Comm., Formal Op. 115 (2007).

In direct response to the Colorado opinion, the ABA issued an opinion shortly after, concluding that collaborative law is not per se unethical and does not create a conflict of interest if the client gives informed consent. "Before representing a client in a collaborative law process, a lawyer must advise the client of the benefits and risks of participation in the process. If the client has given his or her informed consent, the lawyer may represent the client in the collaborative law process. A lawyer who engages in collaborative resolution processes still is bound by the rules of professional conduct, including the duties of competence and diligence." See Formal Opinion 07-447, Ethical Considerations in Collaborative Law Practice, ABA Standing Committee on Ethics and Professional Responsibility, August 9, 2007.

All states to consider the issue other than Colorado have aligned with the American Bar Association.

RESOURCES

Robert F. Cochran, Jr., *Legal Ethics and Collaborative Practice Ethics*, 38 HOFSTRA L. REV. 537 (2009).

Christopher M. Fairman, *Growing Pains: Collaborative Law and the Challenge of Legal Ethics*, 30 CAMPBELL L. REV. (2008).

Draft, *Summary of Ethics Rules Governing Collaborative Practice,* ABA Collaborative Law Committee, Ethics Subcommittee (October 10, 2009), available at https/globalcollaborativelaw.com/wp-content/uploads/2017/07/EthicsPaper20091010

APPENDIX A

CASE NAME	LENGTH OF MARRIAGE	AGE & CHILDREN	FAULT	INCOME	PROPERTY DIVISION	ALIMONY	CHILD SUPPORT	APPEAL	COMMENTS
I. Marriages over 20 years									
A. Permanent alimony awarded									
Williamson v. Williamson, 296 So. 3d 206 (Miss. Ct. App. 2020)	21	2 minor children (wife)	Irreconcilable differences	Husband: $8,617./mo; Wife: $1,384/mo	Wife: Approx $230,000	$1200/mo 22% of disparity	$1,720	Husband, aff'd	Wife unable to meet expenses; marriage ended with his affair; Husband had $180,000 in separate property
D. All alimony denied									
Coleman v. Coleman, 324 So. 3d 1204 (Miss. Ct. App. 2021)	20	Husband: disabled; No children	Irreconcilable differences	Husband: $1,500 Soc. Sec./mo; Wife: $2,781/mo	Equal	Denied	NA	Husband, aff'd	Property division provided adequately for both
Neely v. Neely, 305 So. 3d 164 (Miss. Ct. App. 2020)	42	Children emancipated	Irreconcilable differences	Unclear; incomes equal	Unclear	Denied	NA	Husband, aff'd	Equal incomes; neither had debt; parties kept finances separate during marriage
II. Marriages 10 - 19 years									
A. Permanent alimony awarded									
Oates v. Oates, 291 So. 3d 803 (Miss. Ct. App. 2020)	16	Wife, disabled; No children	H: Adultery Wife: disabled	Husband: $33,000/yr.; Unclear		$504/mo (18% of disparity)	NA	Husband, aff'd	Wife unable to work; could not meet expenses
Gaskin v. Gaskin, 304 So. 3d 641 (Miss. Ct. App. 2020)	18	Wife: disabled; 2 minor children (wife)	H: Adultery	Husband: $12,085; Wife: $500/mo	Equal; Wife received $786,521	$1,000/mo (11% of disparity)	$2,417	Husband, aff'd	Wife disabled; substantial disparity
Ewing v. Ewing, 301 So. 3d 709 (Miss. Ct. App. 2020)	15	4 children (wife)	Irreconcilable differences	Husband: $4,752; Wife: $3,115/mo	Wife: $44,000	$500/mo (71% of disparity)	$938/mo	Husband, aff'd	Wife unable to meet expenses; custody of four children
Descher v. Descher, 304 So. 3d 620 (Miss. Ct. App. 2020)	17	2 children (wife)	Irreconcilable differences	Husband: $71,377/mo; Wife: $2,000/mo earning capacity	Equal: $1.5 million	$7,500/mo (12% of disparity)	$7,500/mo	Husband, aff'd	Extreme income disparity; standard of living of marriage
Wildman v. Wildman, 301 So. 3d 787 (Miss. Ct. App. 2020)	15	H: 39; Wife: 38; 2 children (wife)	Irreconcilable differences	Husband: $10,049; Wife: $1,726/mo higher earning capacity	Equal: $198,277	$3,000/mo (46% of disparity)	$1,800/mo	Husband, rev'd	Affirming permanent alimony but reversing amount as excessive; wife could increase earnings by working full-time
B. Rehabilitative alimony awarded									
Warren v. Rhea, 318 So. 3d 1187 (Miss. Ct. App. 2021)	15	1 child (husband)	W: Habitual cruelty	Husband: $4,795; Wife: $2,115	Unclear	$750/mo for 4 yrs (28% of disparity)	None	Husband, rev'd on other grounds	Disparity in incomes
D. All alimony denied									
Pace v. Pace, 324 So. 3d 369 (Miss. Ct. App. 2021)	14	Wife: 43; 1 child (wife)	H: Adultery	Both currently unemployed; both with earning capacity	Wife: $720,000	Denied	$1,200	Wife: aff'd	Wife was young with earning capacity as Dietician; physician husband relinquished license after treatment for addiction
III. Marriages under 10 years NO CASES									
IV. Reversals; type required not clear									
Hammond v. Hammond, 327 So. 3d 173 (Miss. Ct. App. 2021)	25	Wife: 47; 1 child (wife)	Husband: Adultery	Husband: $12,150/mo plus bonus; Wife: $646/mo	Wife: 55%	$500/mo for 2 years (5% of disparity)	$1167/mo	Wife, rev'd	Grossly inadequate considering marriage length, great disparity in incomes; husband's affair ended marriage

Made in the USA
Columbia, SC
23 June 2022

62031289R00093